Contributors

Alice Welch	Jessica Palmer
Angela Tuffy	Iill Leigh
Angus Sutherland	Joanne Cerrone
Anne Leva	Julian Baker
Ashley Young	Julie Hollis
Bernadette McDonnell	Katie Laurie
Carmel Carnegie	Kylie Townsend
Carol Dixon	Lisa Fox
Carol Rea	Lynn Brent
Celine Couchman	Mary Powell
Charmaine Kerr	Matthew Sutherland
Debby Sustins	Meghan Macleod
Deborah Hooker	Monica Hyder
Diane Merry	Niamh McDonnell
Dilys Webb	Priscila Zanuzzo
Donna Harrison	Rachel McDonnell
Fiona Barnes	Rebecca Stokes
Gemma Lago	Richard Tompkins
Geraldine O Gorman	Ross Sutherland
Harry Byers	Sara Gardiner
Iain Sutherland	Sara Hewitt
Ian Stephens	Tabitha Byers
Janine Tompkins	Vivian Curtin
Jennifer Palmer	Zena Cooper

COPYRIGHT

This paperback edition published in 2022 by Jasami Publishing Ltd
an imprint of Jasami Publishing Ltd
Glasgow, Scotland
https://jasamipublishingltd.com

ISBN 978-1-913798-61-1

Copyright © Ruth Denzey 2022

Visit JasamiPublishingLtd.com to read more about all our books and to purchase them. You will also find features, author information and news of any events, also be the first to hear about our new releases.

Vol II
Spring/Summer Recipes

Jasami Publishing
Acknowledgements

The Jasami team is integral in the production of all of our titles, as they are talented, creative and hardworking. Thank you to the following for your work and dedication to this special project. A special thank you to Ruth Denzey's granddaughter for designing the cover illustrations.

Editors

Douglas O'Hara & Aria Tsvetanova

Proof Editor

Maria Rasinkangas

Cover Illustrations

Isabelle Daynes

Chef Ruth Denzey

Dedication

This is dedicated to my family and friends for their continued support through the ups and downs of my fight with cancer.

Acknowledgements

I have spent my life cooking and creating dishes, but never imagined I would write a cookbook. I guess I have the Covid pandemic to thank for getting me started on collating my recipes and doing something positive with them.

I should thank my daughter Meghan for persuading me to get them all down on paper so that she had all her favourite recipes when I'm gone, and my son Alex who has strong opinions on what works and what does not.

My good friends Lynn and Tony Brent and my friend Julie Hollis who put up with me trying the recipes out on them and the many others who have tried them.

My friend Celine Delille who helped me start to edit the many pages into some semblance of order. Sally Macleod who liked the initial idea so much that she introduced me to the marvellous Michele of Jasami Publishing and then Douglas and Aria who spent hours correcting my mistakes and editing it all as well as Maria's proofreading skills.

Thanks to all my Facebook followers who liked my page so much they have enabled me to crowdfund (through Crowdbound) the book and last but most important of all the amazing chemo staff at the Celia Blakey cancer unit for their amazing work, along with all the fabulous Macmillan nurses, and the Celia Blakey Unit who make having cancer that bit more bearable.

Table of Contents

Starters
and
Light Bites

CREAMY ONION SOUP
WITH WILD GARLIC AND WALNUT PESTO

2 banana shallots, sliced

2 medium onions, sliced

1 leek, sliced

2-4 spring onions, chopped

1 large garlic clove

50g butter

Sprig of thyme

150ml white wine

300-400ml milk

A good splash of double cream

"I fancied soup for lunch so raided the veg drawer for stuff that needed using up. I found half a bunch of spring onions, a leek, a couple of banana shallots and a couple of onions that had all seen slightly better days. Maybe I should call it rapscallion soup... Feel free to use any combination you have or make it with about the same amount of onion only.
My usual place for wild garlic is not as abundant this year as it's being swamped with ivy. If you know somewhere to find it, I recommend making this pesto; it has so many uses!"

Serves 3-4

WILD GARLIC PESTO

100g wild garlic, washed

80g walnuts

Juice of 1/2 to 1 lemon

60g parmesan, grated

150ml olive oil

Salt and pepper

Melt the butter in a saucepan and add all the onions/leeks etc. with a good sprinkle of salt, which helps the onion to soften. Cook slowly over low to medium heat about 20 minutes, until all are soft and melty. Add the garlic and continue to cook until softened. Add the wine, milk and thyme and bring to a boil. Simmer for another 20 minutes and then puree with a hand blender or in a food processor. Add the cream and some black pepper. Serve with the pesto, or chive oil.

Put the wild garlic, walnuts and lemon juice in a food processor and pulse until almost smooth but with some texture. Drizzle in the oil whilst running to make a nice paste but with some texture. Add the grated parmesan and salt and pepper and mix quickly.

Serve with the soup, or with pasta, or chicken. Or use in any recipe which requires pesto.

FRESH ASPARAGUS SOUP

"As the asparagus season draws to an end, it gets cheaper and often you can get bunches of imperfect or skinny stalks which are perfect for soup. A little tip - I keep a pack of instant potato mash in the cupboard for when I am making soup. If it comes out too thin, I can stir some in as a thickener..."

Serves 2

2 bunches of asparagus
1 medium shallot, or green part of a leek, or 1/2 large onion
40g butter

1 vegetable or chicken stock cube/pot
Instant potato to thicken, if necessary
Salt, pepper and double cream

If the asparagus stalks look particularly woody at the ends, remove this bit and discard. Cut just the tips off and keep. Dice the rest of the stalk and slice the onion/leek/shallot.

Melt the butter and add the vegetables (not the asparagus tips). Stir till the onion has softened. Add the stock cube and just cover it with water. Bring to a boil then turn down and simmer until asparagus is just soft.

Blend really well with a hand blender or processor and if desired, pass through a sieve but hopefully it shouldn't need it. Add the tips back in and cook for a further 3-5 minutes. If necessary, thicken with a little potato powder.

Pour into bowls and garnish with cream.

Authentic Falafels

and Roast Garlic Hummus

"Bit of a chickpea fest today, sunny weather food. You do need to think about the falafel the night before and soak the chickpeas."

Makes about 20

FALAFEL
250g dried chickpeas, soaked in cold water overnight then drained
1 small onion, roughly chopped
Zest of 1 lemon
1-2 red chillies, chopped
1 tsp ground cumin
2 tsp ground coriander
Handful fresh coriander
Handful fresh parsley
3 garlic cloves
1 tsp salt
2 Tbsp gram flour or plain flour
1 tsp baking powder
1 egg

HUMMUS
1 tin chickpeas
Zest and juice of a lemon
1 chilli, chopped
Handful fresh coriander
Handful fresh parsley
1/2 small garlic head (3-4 large garlic cloves)
Salt and pepper
Good olive oil

Pop the garlic in the oven and roast for 20-30 minutes until soft, golden, and jammy. Peel and put in a processor with all the other ingredients except olive oil. Puree well and then slowly add some ice-cold water until light creamy consistency.
Tip into a bowl and drizzle with good olive oil. Serve with flatbreads or crusty bread.

Place all ingredients except the baking powder in a food processor and mix until almost a puree, but still with a little texture. Tip into a bowl and refrigerate for 1-2 hours. When ready to cook, add the baking powder and mix well. Shape into about 20 balls and flatten slightly into discs. Fry over medium heat until browned on both sides. Finish in a medium oven for 10-13 minutes.
Serve with mint and garlic yoghurt.

Chickpea Flour Crackers

Gluten-Free

250ml chickpea (besan) flour
1/2 tsp smoked paprika
1/2 tsp dried oregano
1/2 tsp garlic salt
1/4 tsp salt (rock or sea salt)
1 Tbsp olive oil
60ml water

"I made these for dipping, or having with drinks, but you could cut them in larger squares to have with cheese. I served them with a tahini sour cream dip."

Serves 2

Preheat oven to 200°C.

Mix the dry ingredients in a bowl, then add the oil and most of the water. Mix together, adding more water, if necessary, turn out of the bowl and knead to make a soft pliable dough.

Roll out the dough between 2 sheets of baking parchment as thinly as possible, about 3 to 6mm. Remove the top sheet of parchment, slide the dough onto a baking tray and cut into the shapes you want.

Sprinkle with a little more oregano and sea salt. Bake until the crackers are beginning to brown and remove them from the oven. Peel them off the parchment and allow to crisp as they cool.

Serve with a dip - I mixed tahini with sour cream, garlic and lemon juice to taste.

Muhammara

"Yes, another dip, but I'm a bit bored with both the hummus / tzatziki, and everyone loved this change last night at our Eurovision song contest party. You will need a food processor for this recipe."

Serves 8 (as a dip)

250g roasted red peppers from a jar
4 Tbsp good olive oil
4 Tbsp Pomegranate molasses
1 tsp smoked paprika
A big pinch of chilli flakes
80g walnuts
2 handfuls of fresh or frozen breadcrumbs
Salt and pepper

Drain the peppers and chop roughly. Put in the processor with the oil, molasses, paprika, chilli flakes, salt and pepper, and pulse until fairly smooth. Add the walnuts and breadcrumbs and continue to pulse until smooth but with some texture.

Spoon into a bowl and finish with some chopped walnuts, chopped coriander and a drizzle of oil.

Serve with flatbread.

SAVOURY EGG CUSTARD
(OR CRUSTLESS QUICHE)

"Savoury egg custard used to be invalid food and quite unappealing, but I love quiche. So, when using up egg yolks and bits in the fridge, I made this, and really quite like it. It's also gluten-free and carb-free. A good, very quick light lunch or supper."

Makes 2

6 slices salami
2 egg yolks
150ml double cream
2 Tbsp spinach, cooked, chopped and well-drained
3-4 sun-dried tomatoes, chopped
20g parmesan, grated
Salt and pepper

Lightly oil 2 deep ramekins and line with 3 salami slices in each.

Beat the egg yolks and cream together and season well. Add the chopped, well-squeezed spinach, the sun-dried tomatoes and the parmesan. Mix well and divide between the 2 ramekins.

Bake in a preheated heated oven, at 200°C for around 20 minutes until the egg has risen slightly and browned but is still a bit wobbly in the middle.

BURRATA, PESTO, AND TOMATO SALAD

"This is delicious on a hot summers day for lunch. Best made when tomatoes are in season and full of flavour. You can get burrata from Waitrose, and I have seen it in Tesco before."

Serves 2

I fresh burrata cheese
50g pine nuts + extra for garnish
50g parmesan cheese grated
80g fresh basil

2 garlic cloves
150ml good olive oil
Salt and pepper
4 large ripe tomatoes
or selection of heritage tomatoes

Slice the tomatoes and spread evenly onto the plate in a circle.
Toast the pine nuts in a small frying pan.
Put 50g of pine nuts and the garlic in a processor or pestle and mortar and blend. Add the basil and parmesan and blend again. Slowly add the oil to make a smooth creamy sauce and season to taste.
Cut the burrata in 1/2 and divide between the two plates. Drizzle over the pesto, sprinkle on the extra whole pine nuts, and grate over some more parmesan cheese. Drizzle with some extra virgin olive oil and sprinkle some black pepper.
Serve with thinly sliced and toasted sourdough.

Griddled Peach, Serrano Ham,
Feta, and Walnut Salad

"It's so hot today, it had to be salad! A friend gave me some lovely Turkish cheese, the name of which escapes me. It is not easy to acquire but pretty similar to feta."

Serves 4

6 ripe peaches or nectarines
8 slices of Serrano ham
1 block feta (200g)
1 bag rocket
Handful of walnuts, toasted

1 Tbsp lemon juice
1/2 Tbsp runny honey
4 Tbsp virgin olive oil
Salt and black pepper

Whisk the lemon juice, honey, oil , salt and pepper together.

Tip the rocket onto a large serving platter. Tear the serrano ham slices in 1/2 and lay around amongst the rocket.

Halve the peaches, remove the stones and heat a griddle. Lightly oil the griddle and cook the peaches cut side down on high heat to char. Lay the peaches amongst the rocket and crumble the feta over everything, along with the toasted chopped walnuts.

Drizzle everything with the dressing and serve.

Leftover BBQ Salad
with Buttermilk Dressing

Leftover BBQ Salad
with Buttermilk Dressing

"With the fabulous weather yesterday we had a barbecue, of course. And, as usual, I was left with a couple of bits of chicken, a couple of half corn on the cobs and a few spears of griddled asparagus. You can use any leftover griddled veg or tinned sweetcorn, fresh tomatoes...whatever you have on hand."

Serves 2

SALAD
1 cooked chicken breast
100g pasta
2 spring onions, sliced
4 rashers streaky bacon, grilled and chopped
Assorted leftover griddled veg, or veg of your choice
Salad leaves

DRESSING
3 Tbsp buttermilk
2 Tbsp mayonnaise
2 Tbsp Greek yoghurt
1 Tbsp chives, chopped
1/2 tsp honey
Squeeze of lemon juice
Salt and pepper

Cook the pasta according to the instructions on the packet. Run under cold water and drain well. Dice the cooked chicken and toss through the pasta with the spring onion, bacon and all your vegetables.

Whisk all the dressing ingredients together and fold through the pasta. Tip onto a bed of salad leaves and dress with edible flowers. I used wild garlic, nasturtium and chive flowers.

Asian Beansprout Salad

"As summer arrives and salad is on everybody's minds, it's hard sometimes not to keep having the usual: coleslaw, potato etc. This one is light and very healthy. You could add toasted sesame seeds, or noodles to make more filling. (But you might need more dressing if using noodles.)"

Serves 2 (as a main) or 4 (as a side)

DRESSING

4 Tbsp olive or sunflower oil

1 tsp sesame oil

SALAD

200g fresh beansprouts

1 Tbsp lemon or lime juice

4 spring onions

2 Tbsp soy sauce

100g button mushrooms, sliced

A pinch of chilli flakes

1/2 red or yellow pepper

1 tsp ginger puree

Fresh coriander, chopped

1/2 tsp garlic puree

In a small bowl, whisk all the dressing ingredients.

Mix all the salad ingredients together in a large bowl and add dressing.

Mix well and serve.

This salad doesn't last and needs eating on the day it is made.

Celeriac Remoulade

"This works best if you use the grater attachment on a food processor, but you can use a normal course grater as well. I won't give exact amounts for the optional extras, just add to taste."

Serves 6

Optional extras:
diced apple, chopped pecans/walnuts, raisins, grated cheese, fresh herbs.

1/2 celeriac, peeled and grated
Juice of 1/2 lemon
Mayonnaise or 1/2 mayonnaise and 1/2 Greek yoghurt
Salt pepper
2 tsp Dijon mustard

As soon as you grate the celeriac, mix with the lemon juice to prevent discolouration. Add enough mayo or mayo-yoghurt to bind and coat the celeriac, add the Dijon and season. Mix in any additional extras.

CHICKEN, WALNUT, AND POMEGRANATE SALAD

"This is really flexible: leave out the chicken to make it vegetarian and you can use a vegan cheese in place of feta. I had leftover roast chicken, but you could pan fry and slice a large chicken breast. It needs lots of herbs, about 40g in whatever ratio you like. I use about 40% parsley, 40% coriander, and 20% mint."

Serves 2

100g bulgur wheat
1/2 chicken or vegetable stock cube
3-4 spring onions
1 small pomegranate
40g total mint, parsley, and coriander
Juice of 1/2 large lemon
2-3 Tbsp good olive oil
Cooked chicken
40g walnuts
40g Greek feta or a vegan alternative
Pomegranate molasses
Salt and pepper

Put the bulgur wheat and the stock cube in a bowl and just cover with boiling water. Allow to soak until the water is absorbed and the bulgur wheat has softened. Allow to cool. Chop spring onions and add them along with lemon juice, oil, herbs, pomegranates seeds, salt, and pepper. Crumble the feta into the bowl and tip into 2 dishes.

Chop the chicken into bite-size pieces and scatter over top. Toast the walnuts in a dry frying pan, chop and scatter over.

Drizzle generously with pomegranate molasses and serve.

Tuna Mayo Potato Salad

"Gone a bit retro today: simple, vibrant and old school salad."

Serves 2

4-6 medium new potatoes, cooked and cooled	100g green beans cooked and cooled
1 can tuna steak	Anchovy fillets, chopped
2 Tbsp mayo	2-3 spring onions
1 Tbsp yoghurt	2 eggs
Juice 1/2 a lemon	Seasoning
6-8 cherry tomatoes	Chopped parsley

Boil the eggs for 7 minutes and cool immediately in cold water. Peel and halve.
Dice the potatoes, cut the beans into chunks and slice the spring onions. Drain the tuna and tip it into a bowl. Add the mayonnaise, yoghurt and lemon juice. Season with salt and pepper. Fold through the potatoes, beans and spring onions. Tip into a dish. Cut the tomatoes into quarters and scatter over them. Lay the eggs on top and scatter over chopped anchovies and chopped parsley.

Panzanella Salad

"This is only worth making in the summer and autumn when local tomatoes are at their best and sweetest. The anchovies are optional but add lots of savoury flavours. Substitute with good black olives, if preferred."

Serves 4

500-600g assorted local tomatoes (different colours is good)
1/2 tsp salt
1 slice sourdough or a ciabatta roll
1/2 tin of anchovies, finely chopped (or black olives)
1 large clove of garlic, finely chopped

1 banana shallot, finely chopped
1-2 Tbsp capers
3-4 Tbsp good olive oil + some for bread
Fresh basil
Ground Black pepper
1/2 tsp dijon mustard

Cut the tomatoes into quarters, halves or any shape and size you fancy. Put in a bowl and add the salt. Stir well and leave to sit for 1 hour or more.

Tear the bread into small chunks and drizzle with olive oil. Bake on a tray in the oven at 200°C for a few minutes until beginning to brown but not too crisp.

Drain the tomatoes in a sieve and keep the juice. Add the anchovies, capers, shallot, garlic and basil. Whisk the juice, olive oil, mustard and pepper together and add to the tomatoes.

Just before serving, add the crisp bread, mix and serve immediately.

COURGETTE AND SMOKED SALMON ROULADE

"This is easily made vegetarian by using olives and feta, and sun-dried tomatoes instead of salmon. Simple to make if you have a whisk. And great if you have a glut of courgettes!"

Serves 8

350-400g grated courgette
5 large eggs
4-5 Tbsp plain flour or gluten-free flour
1/2 tsp garlic powder

50g parmesan, grated
1/2 tsp salt
Black pepper
340g cream cheese
200g smoked salmon
Squeeze of lemon

Preheat the oven to 200°C.

Mix the salt with the courgettes and leave to drain in a sieve.

Separate the eggs being careful not to get any yolk in the white or it will not whisk as well. Squeeze out the courgettes, put them in a bowl and add the egg yolks, garlic powder, pepper, parmesan, and flour. Mix well.

Whisk the egg whites to soft but strong peaks and fold into the courgettes gently so as not to knock out the air.

Line a Swiss roll tin 35 x 25cm with baking parchment. Spread the courgette mixture evenly over and into the corners. Bake for about 15-20 minutes until lightly browned and just firm.

Turn upside down onto another sheet of parchment (you can grate some more parmesan onto this for added flavour). Remove the top parchment carefully and allow to cool slightly before rolling up from the short end. When cool, unroll and spread with the cream cheese and lay salmon slices evenly over, squeeze lemon juice over and re-roll.

PRAWN AND SPINACH ARANCHINI

"A creamy risotto is a thing of beauty, roll it in balls and deep fry and it becomes even more delicious!"

Makes 14-16 balls

1 large banana shallot, finely chopped
1 large clove of garlic, finely chopped
1 Tbsp butter
100ml white wine
200g arborio rice
200g raw shelled prawns

100g fresh spinach
Zest of 1/2 lemon
1 fish stock cube
Salt and black pepper
75g parmesan grated

Melt the butter in a medium saucepan and add the shallots and garlic. Allow to cook until softened and then add the rice. Stir well to coat with butter and then add the wine. Bring to a boil and simmer gently. Add the stock cube, lemon zest, salt, and pepper. As the wine reduces add 300-400ml water a little at a time, reducing each time between additions.

Cook until rice is just cooked but not chalky. Roughly chop the prawns and the spinach and add. Heat just enough to wilt the spinach and just cook the prawns. Add the parmesan and spread it out into a shallow dish to cool. Refrigerate.

Once cold and set, shape into about 14-16 balls. I sometimes freeze them at this point so they are firm, but it is not essential.

Dip the balls in seasoned flour, then the beaten egg then the breadcrumbs.

Fill a large saucepan up to 1/3 with oil and heat until a piece of bread dropped in floats immediately.

Fry the balls a few at a time. Serve warm.

THAI SALMON FISH CAKES

"Light, healthy, and easy to make."

Makes 6

750g fresh salmon, skinned and boned   2 tsp ginger puree
3 spring onions, chopped   1 Tbsp soy sauce
Good handful of fresh coriander   1 Tbsp lemon juice
2 Tbsp Thai red curry paste   2 tsp sesame oil

Chop the salmon into chunks. Put the spring onions and coriander in a food processor and chop roughly. Add the remaining ingredients and pulse until smooth-ish but not puree.

Turn out and shape into 6 cakes. Pan fry until golden brown and just cooked through.

Serve with chilli mayonnaise.

Thai Spiced Mussels

with Irish Soda Bread

"A lovely change from classic mussels in wine, this is a lovely delicate twist."

Serves 2, generously

Thai Spiced Mussels

with Irish Soda Bread

MUSSELS

1kg mussels	1 Tbsp fish sauce
4-5 spring onions	1 Tbsp brown sugar
1 Tbsp Thai green curry paste	1-2 Tbsp lime juice
1 can coconut milk	Chopped coriander

Tip the mussels into very cold water and clean, scrubbing off any grit and pulling off the hairy beards if they have them. Tap any open mussels on the work surface, discarding any that don't close after a few seconds.

In a pan with a lid large enough to take all the mussels, fry the spring onions in a little vegetable oil until softened. Add the curry paste and cook for another minute. Add the coconut milk, fish sauce, brown sugar and lime juice. Simmer for 5 minutes. Add the mussels and put the lid on the pan. Heat quickly until all the mussels are opened.

Serve sprinkled with chopped coriander and lime wedges.

Discard any that haven't opened.

IRISH SODA BREAD

170g white plain flour	280ml buttermilk (or milk with a good
170g wholemeal plain flour	squeeze of lemon, plain yoghurt or a
10g salt	combination)
1 tsp bicarbonate of soda	Jumbo oats

Mix all the dry ingredients except the oats in a bowl and add buttermilk. Mix quickly and lightly. Sprinkle oats over the work surface and turn the dough out onto them. Shape into a ball and flatten slightly. Place on a baking sheet and cut a cross on the top. Bake at 200°C for 20-30 minutes until deep golden brown. The loaf should sound hollow when tapped on the base.

SOUTHERN SPICED FISH NUGGETS

SOUTHERN SPICED FISH NUGGETS

300g thick cod or white fish fillet
75g plain flour
25g cornflour or gluten-free flour
1 large egg
1 Tbsp garlic granules
1 Tbsp English mustard powder
1 Tbsp smoked paprika
1 tsp chilli flakes
1 tsp turmeric
1 tsp dried oregano
Salt and black pepper
Oil for frying

"I got to go to my favourite fishmongers yesterday and went mad so there will be quite a few fish recipes coming up. These are nice in a wrap with coleslaw or celeriac remoulade or just with mixed salad."

Serves 2

Cut the fish into 6-8 chunky pieces.

Beat the egg with a little salt and put it in a shallow dish. Mix all the other ingredients together in a large bowl.

Dip the fish chunks into the flour mixture, then into the egg, and then back into the flour mixture.

If you have a deep fryer, heat it to 180/190°C. Otherwise, fill 1/3 of a deep saucepan or fill a deep frying pan to about 2cm with oil and heat until a small piece of bread dropped in, floats and bubbles.

Carefully drop the fish balls into the oil and cook until deep golden brown. You may have to cook them in batches.

Drain on kitchen paper.

AUBERGINE AND GOAT'S CHEESE SANDWICHES

"I made these delicious crispy indulgences vegetarian using sun-dried tomatoes, but you could add sliced salami, chorizo, parma ham, etc., and use mozzarella or gruyere for a change."

Makes 6

1 large aubergine, cut into 12 discs
180g goat's cheese log
6 sun-dried tomatoes (or alternative)
Seasoned flour

2 eggs
Breadcrumbs (panko are good, I used sourdough)
Vegetarian sunflower oil

Heat oven to 200°C. Slice the goat's cheese into 6 discs and sandwich between the aubergine slices with the sun-dried tomatoes (or alternative). Press firmly. Put the seasoned flour, breadcrumbs and beaten eggs in separate shallow dishes.
Carefully coat each sandwich in flour, then egg, and breadcrumbs as evenly as possible.
Add about 1-2cm of oil to a frying pan big enough to hold the sandwiches. When hot, cook the sandwiches on a medium heat turning once when going brown. Pop into the preheated oven for 10-15 minutes to cook through.
Serve with salad, and maybe sweet chilli sauce.

BEETROOT TARTE TATIN

1 pack ready-rolled puff pastry

400g cooked beetroot, wedged

1 small red onion, sliced

20g butter

30g light brown sugar

30ml balsamic vinegar

1 star anise

Sprig of fresh thyme

Cheese of choice

A few chopped walnuts (optional)

"Normally I would make this with goat's cheese but as I am still raiding the Christmas cheese box I have used Blacksticks Blue. You can make this with a raw beetroot. Just put in the oven for about 15-20 minutes after just bringing beetroot, onion, sugar etc to a boil."

Serves 4

In a frying pan with an approximately 24cm diameter (preferably non-stick or cast iron), melt the butter. Add the sliced red onion and cook until beginning to soften. Add the beetroot, sugar, star anise, thyme and balsamic vinegar. Simmer, stirring occasionally until slightly syrupy. Remove from heat and allow to cool.

Unroll the pastry and cut a circle the same diameter as the frying pan. When the filling is cool, place the pastry circle on top and tuck the edges in. Make a slash in the middle to allow steam to escape.

Bake in an oven preheated to 200°C for around 30 minutes until the pastry is deep golden and very crisp.

Shake the pan gently to ensure the filling is not stuck and very carefully flip the pan upside down onto a serving plate (any liquid will be very hot). Crumble over your choice of cheese and walnuts, if using.

Serve with a dressed salad.

BLOOMING ONION

"I've seen this a few times on the Internet and on cookery programmes so thought I would give it a try. I seasoned my flour with Bhaji spices but you could try middle Eastern or Southern spicing."

1 onion, serves 1

1 medium brown or white onion
Milk
Equal parts gram flour and self-raising flour
Ground cumin
Ground coriander
Turmeric
Smoked paprika
Salt and pepper

Peel the onion but **leave the root on.** Cut the onion from the top down towards the root but not all the way down. The root will hold it all together when frying.
Mix the flours together and add the seasonings of your choice to your taste. Season really well with salt and pepper
Dip the onion in the milk, ensuring it gets right to the centre, then toss in the flour mixture, again making sure it gets right into the centre.
Heat a deep fat fryer (or a deep saucepan large enough to take the onion) 1/3 full of oil. **Be careful** as the oil will rise up when frying so make sure it is deep enough. A piece of bread dropped in should bubble straight away if the oil is hot enough.
Carefully lower the onion into the pan, turning over once or twice to make sure it's cooked to the centre and evenly golden brown. Drain on kitchen paper and serve with a sauce of choice.

CHAR SIU PORK

"Chinese barbecue pork tenderloin, delicious served in bao buns, or with rice and pak choi."

Serves 2

1 pork tenderloin	2 Tbsp hoisin sauce
1 Tbsp vegetable oil	2 Tbsp soy sauce
1 tsp sesame oil	1/2 tsp five spice powder
1 Tbsp light brown sugar	1 tsp minced or pureed garlic
2 Tbsp runny honey	2 tsp minced or pureed ginger

Trim the pork tenderloin of any sinews or fat. Mix all the rest of the ingredients in a bowl or bag big enough to take the pork in one piece. Marinade the pork for 3-4 hours or overnight.

Ideally, place a rack over a roasting tin on which to place the pork. Pour enough water in the tin to fill by 1/3. This will help to keep it moist. If that's not possible, place the pork on foil or parchment paper in a roasting tin. Preheat the oven to 200°C. Drain the pork from the marinade but keep the marinade. Cook the pork for 20 minutes, turning and brushing with the marinade halfway through. After 20 minutes, place the pork under a grill and brush well with more marinade. Grill for 10-15 minutes turning and brushing regularly with marinade until going sticky and slightly charred.

Slice and serve in bao buns or with rice and pak choi.

CHORIZO AND GOAT'S CHEESE PARCELS

"I'm lucky enough to have an amazing Asian food shop at the end of my road where I can get frozen wonton sheets. So, this is a sort of fusion food canapé."

Makes 16 small or 8 large canapés

125g soft goat's cheese
100g cream cheese
1/2 chorizo sausage, finely chopped
1-2 spring onions, finely chopped
2-3 sun-dried tomatoes, chopped
Ground black pepper
Wonton wrappers, 9cm or 12cm.
(The 12cm are easier to work with and make a larger parcel. 9cm ones are best for canapés.)
Melted butter

Beat the cheeses together and then add the chorizo, spring onions, sun-dried tomatoes and ground black pepper. Beat well.

Take one sheet of pastry and put a spoonful of filling in the middle. Run a wet finger around the edges, bring them up together and twist. Continue with the rest of the filling. Place on a baking sheet and brush well with melted butter. Bake at 200°C for about 15-20minutes until golden brown.

Serve warm.

CLASSIC SPANISH TORTILLA

"There's lots of different ways of making tortilla. The classic way doesn't use cooked potatoes but thinly sliced raw potatoes that are almost braised in olive oil with onions and garlic before adding the eggs. You can add other things, but I have just added some baby courgette and fresh herbs."

Serves 4

1 medium brown onion, thinly sliced
500g medium waxy potatoes (like Charlotte)
1 large garlic clove, thinly sliced
80-100ml olive oil
6 large eggs
1-2 small courgettes, finely sliced
Fresh herbs (I used oregano and chives)
Salt and pepper

Thinly slice the potatoes. Heat the oil in a good small (about 20cm) non-stick frying pan and add the onion and potatoes. Stir well and turn the heat down to medium, cover with a lid. Allow to cook, turning over every so often until the potatoes are softened and beginning to colour slightly. Add the courgettes, garlic and herbs and continue cooking for another couple of minutes.

Beat the eggs together and season well. Turn up the heat and add the eggs, giving it all a quick stir. After another couple of minutes, turn the heat down slightly and allow it to begin to set, and colour on the bottom. Pop under a grill to set the top, but you want it still slightly soft in the middle. Turn out upside down onto a serving plate.

You can eat this either hot or cold.

GÖZLEME

SPINACH AND FETTA

"I can't believe I only discovered these amazing and delicious breads 5 years ago, and in Tasmania of all places, when they originate from Turkey."

Makes 2

DOUGH
250g plain flour
125ml Greek yoghurt
100ml cold water
2 tsp olive oil
Salt and pepper

FILLING
300g spinach, wilted and well squeezed
200g feta cheese, crumbled or diced
4 spring onions
6-8 sun-dried tomatoes, chopped (optional)
1 red chilli, finely diced (optional)
Salt and pepper
Olive oil for rolling

Mix together all the dough ingredients, adding a little extra water if needed and knead until smooth and elastic. If it's too wet, add a little more flour but only enough to stop it sticking. Alternatively, use a stand mixer. Leave to rest in bowl for 1 hour or so.

Chop the spinach fairly small and then chop the spring onions. Mix together with all the other filling ingredients.

Divide the dough into 2 and, using oil on the counter, roll or push the dough into a square approximately 25-30cm. Spread 1/2 the filling mix in the middle into a square with points in the middle of the long sides. Fold the corners over like an envelope to enclose the filling. Press gently. Heat a large fry pan with a little oil to cover the bottom. Carefully lift the gözleme into it. Fry on one side for around 5 minutes then carefully turn over and repeat, pressing down gently to remove air pockets.

Turn onto a board and cut into squares or wedges.

SHAKSHUKA

"A great lunch, brunch or light dinner recipe, vegetarian and carb-free."

Serves 4

2 Tbsp olive oil	Harissa paste to taste
1 large onion, thinly sliced	2 Tbsp tomato puree
1 red or yellow pepper, sliced	2 400g tins tomatoes, chopped
2 garlic cloves, chopped	8 eggs
1/2 tsp cumin seeds	100g feta cheese
1/2 tsp smoked paprika	Salt and pepper
1/2 tsp caraway seeds	Chopped coriander

Fry the onion and pepper in the olive oil until soft and colouring. Add the garlic, spices and harissa. Cook for a few moments then add the puree and tinned tomatoes and cook slowly over medium heat until thickened. About 10 minutes. Stir in coriander, salt, and pepper.

Make small wells in the sauce and break an egg into each hole, cover with a lid and cook on a low heat until the eggs are cooked and how you like them. Sprinkle crumbled feta over. You can transfer the sauce to a baking dish and bake in the oven with a lid on rather than on the hob.

The sauce also freezes well in portions so that you can defrost and cook one at a time.

HOMEMADE POTATO GNOCCHI

"I'm going, to be honest: this is not a recipe I would do when I come home from a hard day at work. But on a lockdown Monday or weekend, it's fun! I made a sun-dried tomato, chorizo and spinach sauce, but it is easily adapted. Suggestions are at the end."

Serves 4

HOMEMADE POTATO GNOCCHI

GNOCCHI

2 very large (500g) floury potatoes	1 large egg
120g plain flour	Salt and pepper

Bake the potatoes. I find it best to first microwave them for 10 minutes or so and then put in a hot oven until well cooked. You can use boiled potatoes, but you want them as dry as possible. I've seen suggestions using leftover mash, but if, like me, you add loads of butter and cream to your mash, the gnocchi might fall apart when cooking.

Either dice the potatoes or mash them. I very quickly whisked them to break up. You want to keep it as light as possible with no lumps. Add the flour and the beaten egg and mix as quickly and as lightly as possible.

Turn out onto the worktop and kneed gently, just enough to bring it together.; it should not be sticky. Add a little more flour, if necessary. Do not overwork! Divide into 4 pieces and, using a little flour to dust the surface, roll into long thin sausages and cut into even pieces. Repeat with the other pieces. Place them on a baking tray with baking parchment and a dusting of flour or semolina. Leave for 20 minutes minimum.

When ready to cook, drop into plenty of salted boiling water and cook until they all float to the surface. Check one by cutting it in 1/2 to see that it's just cooked. Add to the sauce of your choice.

SAUCE - 2 portions

1/2 a small onion, finely chopped	2 handfuls of fresh spinach, chopped
1/2 a chorizo, chopped small	Splash of wine
6-8 sun-dried tomatoes, chopped	150-200ml double cream

In a small frying pan, lightly brown the chorizo, then add the onions and garlic and cook until softened. Add a splash of wine, tomatoes and spinach. Cook until the spinach has wilted and only a little liquid is left. Add the cream and bring it to a boil. Simmer until the sauce is a coating consistency.

Most of the ingredients can be substituted with other ingredients (see below). The basic formula is: pan fry ingredients, add wine, reduce, add cream and any cheeses.

Other options:
Spinach, blue cheese and walnut, cream, bacon, mushroom, tomato, butternut squash, chestnut, and bacon

Spanakopita

"I had my vegetarian daughter coming to my bubble tonight for drinks and film, so made these. They reheat well."

Makes about 6 starter size or 1 large

200g fresh or frozen leaf spinach, wilted or defrosted and very well squeezed
200g feta cheese
1 small onion, finely chopped
1 garlic clove, grated or very finely chopped
A good pinch of dried oregano

Chopped fresh mint or a good pinch, dried
25g pinenuts
Salt and pepper
A little olive oil
6-10 sheets filo pastry
Melted butter

Roughly chop the spinach and put it in a bowl. Heat a little oil in a frying pan and add the onions. Cook until softened, add the garlic and cook for a little longer. Tip the onions into the spinach. Add herbs and seasoning, pine nuts, and crumbled feta.

Take one sheet of filo and brush it with melted butter. Take about 1/6 of the mix and place it in a sausage shape towards one corner. Fold over the corner, then both edges and roll. Repeat with the rest of the mix and place on a baking sheet. Brush with more butter and bake at 200°C until golden brown.

You can make one big one by brushing 4 sheets of filo and pushing it into an 18cm sandwich cake tin. Fill with spinach mixture, spreading out evenly. Fold the edges over. Brush more sheets of filo and crumple up on the top. Bake at 200°C until golden brown.

STUFFED MUSHROOMS

"This is a very flexible recipe. You can substitute or add so many different ingredients! I am giving you what I used, but will list other options at the end. I always keep breadcrumbs in the freezer, I make them with stale bread to use as and when. This is great for clearing out odds and ends in the fridge!"

Serves 4 (as a starter)

4 large flat-field mushrooms
1 small onion, finely chopped
2 garlic cloves, crushed
Cured meat (I used some salami and ham, chopped)
200g fresh spinach
4-5 sun-dried tomatoes, chopped

80-100g breadcrumbs (about 2 good handfuls)
150g cheese of choice (stilton, cheddar, smoked, gruyere, or mozzarella)
A knob of butter
Salt and pepper

Wilt the spinach in the microwave for a minute or so, or pour over boiling water to wilt. Squeeze out well and chop. Rub the outside of the mushrooms with a little oil or butter, remove the stems and keep them.

In a small frying pan cook the onions and garlic in a little butter until soft. Add the meat (if using) and chopped mushroom stems and brown lightly. Add the spinach and tomatoes then the breadcrumbs. Tip into a bowl and season. When cool, add the cheese and mix well. Pile into the mushrooms and top with extra cheese. Bake at 200°C until the cheese has melted and browned, and the mushrooms are piping hot.

Other options: bacon, chorizo, peppers, chilli, kale, celery, cooked lentils, cooked chicken, spring onions.

STUFFED COURGETTE FLOWERS
WITH HONEY

"This is, without doubt, a fiddly dish, but if you're growing courgettes, it is worth a try. I suggest picking the flowers when they are open and stuffing them as it is really difficult to unravel them to stuff when closed. I also decided to do them in breadcrumbs, as they can be shallow fried, but you can do them in light batter and deep fry them."

75g goat's cheese
75g cream cheese
1-2 Tbsp pine nuts, toasted
Sprig of thyme, chopped
Salt and pepper
Flour

1 egg, beaten
Breadcrumbs
6 courgette flowers
Oil for frying
Runny honey

Serves 2

Mash together the 2 kinds of cheese, then add the pine nuts and thyme. Open the flowers and remove the stamen. Split the cheese between them and wrap the petals around, twisting the ends to seal. Toss in flour, then beaten egg, and then the breadcrumbs (you can add grated parmesan for extra flavour, if liked). Ensure the flowers are evenly coated.

Heat the oil until a piece of bread dropped in floats and sizzles, and then fry the flowers, turning regularly until evenly deep golden colour. Drain well on kitchen paper and serve drizzled with honey

STICKY CHINESE PORK BELLY

"You need a small casserole with a lid that will just take the belly slices."

Serves 2

GLAZE
2 Tbsp soy sauce
2 Tbsp honey
1/2 Tbsp ginger puree
1 Tbsp brown sugar
Pinch chilli flakes or chopped red chilli
1/2 Tbsp sesame oil
Sesame seeds

PORK BELLY
500g pork belly slices
Braising liquor
1 tsp ginger puree
1 tsp garlic puree
1 star anise
1 chicken or vegetable stock cube

Put the ingredients for braising liquor in the casserole, add some boiling water and the belly slices. The liquid should just cover the slices. Braise in a medium oven until tender, about 1 hour to 1 hour 30 minutes.
Remove belly and allow to cool. Strain the liquor and keep.
Once cool, cut the belly into chunks. Heat a little oil in a frying pan and fry the chunks until coloured all over. Remove. Mix the glaze ingredients except for the sesame seeds and add them to the pan. Add some of the stock and then reduce the liquid until it is slightly thickened. Add the belly pieces back in and continue to cook until the sauce is going sticky and coating the pork.
Serve sprinkled with sesame seeds.

Sweet Potato Fritters with
Harissa Yoghurt and Poached Egg (GF-VEG)

"At the end of the recipe there will be suggestions for other variations."

Serves 4

FRITTERS
400g sweet potato, peeled and grated
3-4 spring onions, chopped
150g gluten-free flour (you can use plain flour or mix it with gram flour)
3 egg whites
2 tsp harissa paste (or to taste)
1 Tbsp parsley, chopped
2 tsp garlic granules (optional)
Salt and pepper to taste

4 eggs
200g Greek yoghurt
50g harissa paste

In a large bowl, mix all the fritter ingredients together adding a little cold water if necessary to loosen the mixture slightly. Allow to sit for a little while and then shape into 8 to 12 patties depending on what size you like.

Heat a little oil in a frying pan and cook in batches for about 2 to 3 minutes on each side until browned and cooked through, turning the heat down if they brown too quickly. Keep warm on a tray in the oven.

Meanwhile, bring a saucepan of water to a boil, add 2 Tbsp of vinegar and when boiling turn down the heat then drop in the 4 eggs to poach. Poach until cooked but yolks are still soft.

Divide yoghurt between 4 plates and split harissa between each plate. Muddle with the end of a knife to give a marbling effect then stack fritters with egg on top. sprinkle with more parsley or other herbs.

This works well with grated carrot, cumin seeds, ground coriander and chopped coriander in place of sweet potato and harissa. Great served with griddled halloumi, grilled bacon, avocado and chicken. Endless possibilities! Or part cook cauliflower florets, chop roughly but small and use in place of sweet potato.

PICNIC LOAF

"Fabulous weather all week, so we decided to picnic on Sunday....and then it tipped down. Still, I made this which is great for a picnic. I used a Grand mange loaf, a giant baguette, but you could use a normal baguette or some ciabatta. You can pull out some of the soft insides of the bread if you don't want it too doughy. Hard to give quantities as it will depend on what size your loaf is, but the method is the same. Any leftovers are great baked...."

Serves 8-10 (if using grand mange)

1 grand mange, baguette or ciabatta	Pitted olives
2-3 Tbsp mayonnaise	1-2 mozzarella balls, sliced
2-3 Tbsp pesto (I used the wild garlic pesto that I made)	Grated parmesan or cheddar
	Fresh basil
Roasted peppers from a jar, drained	Combination of any of the following: salami
Sun-dried tomatoes chopped	slices, cooked chicken, sliced ham, Parma
Fresh sliced tomatoes	ham, mortadella or anchovies, tuna, prawns

Split the bread lengthways and put it in a hot oven for a few minutes to crispen up slightly. Allow to cool. Meanwhile, mix the mayonnaise and pesto together.

Spread both sides of the bread with the mayonnaise mix. On the bottom 1/2 of the bread layer up all your fillings, seasoning lightly as you go.

Replace the two halves of the bread and press down firmly. Wrap tightly in cling film and leave in the fridge overnight to allow flavours to develop.

Serve sliced in chunks.

Tomato Gruyère Tarts

Tomato Gruyère Tarts

"I made these with my grandsons yesterday, and they are one of the first things my daughter learned to make. I nearly didn't add them here as they are so simple but they are very tasty and you can make smaller ones as canapés."

Makes 10

1 pack ready-rolled puff pastry
Dijon mustard
6-8 ripe tomatoes, sliced

80-100g gruyere cheese, grated
Chopped chives or basil
Salt and pepper

Preheat the oven to 220°C.

Unroll the pastry and cut it in 1/2 lengthways, then cut each 1/2 into 5 rectangles, making 10 in total.

Place the squares on 2 baking trays and spread a little Dijon mustard on each one, leaving a small border. Place 3-4 slices of tomato down the centre of each and season with salt and pepper. Sprinkle with herbs and then top with the cheese, again, making sure you keep a small border.

Bake for about 10 -15 minutes, turning the oven down if they brown too quickly.

Serve with dressed salad.

SPINACH AND SUN-DRIED TOMATO

CHEESECAKE

"This savoury cheesecake is great as a starter or light summer lunch. You could double the cheese mix for a deeper cheesecake and you could substitute or add flavours: blue cheese and walnut work well, or finely chopped smoked salmon. Nothing too wet or it won't set properly."

Serves 6

75g butter, melted

180g digestives or crackers, crushed

50g grated parmesan

400g cream cheese

125g spinach, wilted & squeezed really well

6-8 sun-dried tomatoes

2 large whole eggs + 1 yolk

200ml double cream

100g strong cheese

A pinch of chilli flakes

Salt and black pepper

Butter and baseline a 22cm springform tin with baking parchment. Preheat oven to 160°C.

Melt the butter, add the crushed biscuits and parmesan, and then press into the base of the tin. Bake for around 10 minutes until lightly browned.

Beat the cream cheese, cream, eggs, chilli and salt and pepper together. Chop the spinach and tomatoes, and fold into the cheese mix with the Comte or other cheese. Pour into the tin and bake for about 30-40 minutes until set and lightly coloured with a little wobbly in the middle.

Cool in the tin and serve with salad.

GOAT'S CHEESE MOUSSE
WITH BEETROOT AND CANDIED WALNUTS

*"Great summer lunch, especially if you are growing your own beetroot!
Heritage beetroot in different colours would be even nicer...."*

Serves 6

500-600g beetroot, cooked and peeled
A good handful of walnuts
Caster sugar

MOUSSE:
1 x 120g goats cheese log
100g cream cheese
4-5 Tbsp double cream
Juice of 1/2 a lemon
Salt and pepper
1 tsp hot horseradish sauce (optional)

Put all the mousse ingredients into a food processor and pulse until completely smooth. You could probably do this with a hand blender if necessary.

Put the walnuts in a sieve and run briefly under cold water. Shake well and tip onto a baking tray. Sprinkle generously with caster sugar and bake for 5 minutes, or so, in a medium-hot oven until nicely candied but not too brown. Keep an eye on them!

Slice the beetroot onto 6 individual plates or one large one. Put the mousse into a piping bag and pipe it onto plates, or spoon tidily.

Sprinkle with the candied walnuts and drizzle with good olive oil and balsamic glaze.

DEEP FRIED EGG

"This is just a little additional recipe. I had to soft boil some eggs for scotch eggs and had a couple spare so I did this. You can do this with poached eggs instead."

Serves 2

2 eggs (boiled or poached)   1 egg, beaten (for coating)
Flour   Breadcrumbs
Salt and pepper   Oil, for frying

Using room temperature eggs, drop gently into simmering water and cook for 6 minutes. Plunge immediately into iced water.

Peel carefully, they will be quite fragile. Season some plain flour really well and gently toss the eggs in it. Then dip in beaten egg to cover completely, then in breadcrumbs. You can repeat the egg and breadcrumbs again for an even crisper coat. You could add finely grated parmesan to the breadcrumbs.

Carefully lower into hot oil and cook for about 1-2 minutes until just golden brown and warm. Do not overcook or the yolk will go hard.

I served with bubble and squeak.

Coconut Prawns with Mango Mayo

"I would have liked to find bigger prawns - the larger, the juicier - but these still worked quite well!"

Serves 2 (or 4 as part of meze)

200g fresh or defrosted peeled jumbo prawns
Plain flour
Salt and pepper
Desiccated coconut
Panko or fresh breadcrumbs

1 egg
4 Tbsp Mayonnaise
2 Tbsp mango chutney
1 tsp curry paste
Good squeeze lime juice
Oil for frying

Pat the prawns dry on some kitchen paper. Season the plain flour well with salt and pepper and toss the prawns in it. Beat a large egg in a shallow bowl. Mix equal amounts of desiccated coconut and breadcrumbs together in another shallow bowl. Dip the prawns a few at a time in the beaten egg, and then the breadcrumb mix. Fill a medium saucepan 1/3 full of vegetable oil and heat until a cube of bread dropped into it floats. Cook the prawns a few at a time on medium heat. Drain on kitchen paper and keep warm.

For the dip:

If the mango chutney is chunky, chop it finely. Mix it with the mayo, curry paste and lime.

Serve and enjoy!

CHEESE BEIGNETS

"Little deep-fried cheesy choux puffs, good as nibbles with drinks. You can use any cheese (cheddar, brie, goat's, blue) and add other flavourings (finely chopped sun-dried tomatoes, crispy bacon, spinach, chives, nuts, etc.). I made brie and bacon, and cheddar with sun-dried tomatoes.

Makes about 40-50

280ml water	113g cheese of choice	1 tsp French mustard
113g butter cut into cubes	4 large eggs	Salt and pepper
141g plain flour	Flavouring - bacon bits, nuts etc	Oil for frying

Put the water in a medium saucepan with the butter and bring to a boil until the butter is melted. Add the flour and beat hard and fast until incorporated and smooth. It will look lumpy to start but if you beat it hard, it should go smooth and come away from the sides of the pan. Remove from the heat and add the cheese, mustard, salt, and pepper. Add the eggs one at a time, beating well between each. Add the flavour of your choice.

Heat about 2 inches of oil in a large saucepan or deep fryer, and fry small spoonfuls over medium heat, a few at a time until golden brown and cooked in the middle. Drain on kitchen paper and sprinkle with finely grated parmesan. Serve immediately or cool and freeze to pop in the oven when wanted.

Akoori

Indian Spiced Eggs

"A great brunch dish, a twist on scrambled eggs but not too spicy or hot."

Serves 1-2

1 small green chilli, finely sliced (seeds removed, if preferred)

1 spring onion, finely sliced

1 Tbsp red pepper, finely chopped (optional)

3-4 cherry tomatoes, chopped small

1/2 tsp ground cumin

1/2 tsp turmeric

1/2 tsp ginger puree

1/2 tsp garlic puree

4 eggs

Salt, black pepper,

Chopped coriander

Butter

Small naan bread

Spread the naan with butter and put it in a hot oven.

Melt a knob of butter in a non-stick saucepan and add the chilli, pepper, and spring onion. Cook until softened. Add the cumin and turmeric, ginger and garlic. Cook for a minute and then add the tomatoes. Beat the eggs and season. Add to the saucepan and stirring continuously, cook until the eggs are just cooked but still soft. Stir in the coriander and serve on the hot naan bread.

You could add a little double cream at the end to make it even more unctuous.

Confit Tandoori Chickpeas
with Yoghurt Flatbread and Yoghurt Dressing

"I can't take full credit for this recipe, Yotam Ottolenghi did it on Saturday Kitchen. I have adapted it slightly and the flatbreads are my recipe."

Serves 4

CONFIT TANDOORI CHICKPEAS
WITH YOGHURT FLATBREAD AND YOGHURT DRESSING

1 heaped tsp ground coriander

1 heaped tsp ground cumin

2 x 400g tins chickpeas, drained

10 large garlic cloves, peeled (yes, really, trust me!)

2 tsp ginger puree

300g cherry tomatoes

2-3 red chillies, split lengthways

1 Tbsp tomato puree

1/2 tsp turmeric

2 tsp sweet paprika

1 heaped tsp light brown sugar

200ml olive oil

Salt and pepper

Mix all the ingredients together in an ovenproof casserole with a lid. Cook at 160°C for 75-90 minutes stirring halfway through, until chilli's soft and everything is unctuous. I know it seems like a huge amount of oil but that's the nature of confit. Drain most off before serving and use to cook other spicy dishes.

DRESSING

Juice of 1/2 lime

A good handful of fresh mint

A good handful of fresh coriander

1 garlic clove

200ml Greek yoghurt

Blend all together in a processor or with a hand blender until the herbs and the garlic well-chopped.

FLATBREAD

140g Plain flour

1/2 tsp baking powder

140g Greek yoghurt

Chopped fresh coriander

Salt and pepper

Mix all the ingredients together in a bowl until it is a soft dough. It should be soft but not sticky. Shape into a ball and leave to rest for an hour

Split into 4 pieces and shape each into a ball. Flour the counter and roll out as thinly as possible, about 15cm in diameter.

Heat a non-stick frying pan with a very small knob of butter, and, when sizzling, lay one piece of bread in the pan. When big bubbles start to form, flip it over and cook until browning. Repeat with the rest.

BBQ Corn with Chilli and Parmesan

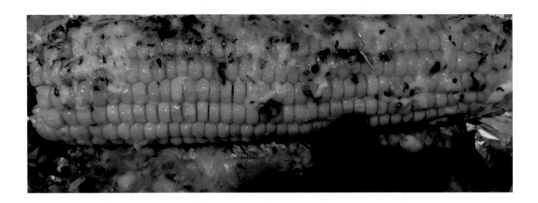

"More sweetcorn today in a really easy recipe that can be roasted in the oven or cooked on the BBQ, if we ever get any sun!!"

Makes 4

4 whole fresh corn on the cob
2 Tbsp butter
Salt and pepper

Dried oregano
4 Tbsp sweet chilli sauce
100g parmesan, grated

Remove the husks from the cobs, if necessary. Rub them all over with the butter and season well with salt, pepper and oregano.

Place on a large sheet of foil and splash with a little water to help steam. Wrap up, not too tightly but well-sealed and place on BBQ or in a hot oven at 200°C.

If barbecuing, cook for about 15 minutes, turning occasionally.

If roasting, roast for about 20 minutes until cooked and steaming.

Open the foil and pour sweet chilli sauce evenly over the corn and sprinkle with cheese.

If barbecuing, pop under a hot grill until cheese is sizzling and brown.

If roasting, put back in the oven until cheese is sizzling and brown

Serve, spooning over the sauce collected in the foil.

INDIAN-SPICED CAULIFLOWER FRITTERS

"Nice little veggie nibbles or side dish. You can also vary the spices to make them Moroccan flavoured or Mexican."

Serves 8

1/2 a large cauliflower, cut into small florets
100g chickpea flour
60g cornflower
1 tsp baking powder
1 tsp garlic granules
1 tsp ground coriander
1 tsp turmeric
1/2 tsp ground cumin

1/2 tsp smoked paprika
Salt and pepper
200ml cold water

OPTIONAL
1/2 tsp Nigella seeds
Pinch chilli flakes
Fresh coriander, chopped

Cook the florets in boiling water for 5 or so minutes until only just soft.
Place the dry ingredients in a bowl and whisk in the water.
Heat 700ml-1 ltr of vegetable oil in a saucepan big enough that the oil comes 1/3 of the way up. Heat to about 160°C or until a small piece of bread, dropped in, rises to the surface immediately. If you have a deep fryer, follow temperature guide. Dip the florets into the batter to coat and fry in small batches.
Serve with a yoghurt dip, or chilli sauce or mango chutney.

Parmigiana

Aubergine, tomatoes, stringy mozzarella, what's not to like! You can add other things too. I like layering Italian salami in it or cooking a couple of chicken breasts and putting in the middle."

Serves 2 (as a main)

1 large aubergine
1 small onion, chopped
1 clove garlic, chopped
2 Tbsp olive oil
2 Tbsp balsamic vinegar
2 tins chopped tomatoes

Splash white wine
Fresh or dried oregano
1 Tbsp tomato puree
1 large or 2 small mozzarella balls
Grated parmesan or cheddar

Slice the aubergine on a slight angle. Mix the oil and vinegar together and brush over both sides and lay on a metal tray in a hot oven until softened and slightly coloured.
Meanwhile, soften the chopped onions in a little oil then add garlic. Cook for another couple of minutes and then add wine, tomatoes, herbs salt and pepper. Simmer for about 30 minutes until the sauce is thick.
Spoon 1/3 sauce into the bottom of the ovenproof dish and add 1/2 the aubergine in a layer. Layer over 1/2 of the mozzarella sliced, then repeat sauce and aubergine. Top with the remaining sauce then remaining mozzarella. Sprinkle over grated cheese and bake at 200ºC until bronze and bubbling.

Main Courses

Salmon Teriyaki

"This also works well with mackerel or chicken."

Serves 4

4 salmon fillets
3 Tbsp soy sauce
3 Tbsp mirin or saki
1/2 tsp chilli flakes or small red chilli, chopped
1/2 tsp grated ginger

1 clove garlic, grated
1 Tbsp sugar
1 lime or 1/2 lemon, squeezed
2 tsp sesame oil (or vegetable oil)
Sesame seeds

Mix all the marinade ingredients together and marinate the salmon for 1 hour. Drizzle the baking tray with a little oil. Remove salmon, sprinkle with sesame seeds, and grill on high heat until sizzling and just cooked. Whilst salmon is grilling, pour marinade into a small saucepan and reduce till slightly syrupy. Pour over grilled fish and serve with rice or noodles.

SMOKEY WHITE FISH AND BEAN STEW

"A light healthy dish, full of flavour."

Serves 4

4 white fish fillets	2 cans of cannellini beans
1 pack streaky bacon or 1 chorizo ring, diced	Juice of 1 lemon
1 medium onion, finely chopped	Olive oil
2 garlic cloves, crushed	Small bag of spinach
1 red chili or pinch chilli flakes	12 (or so) cherry tomatoes,
2 tsp smoked paprika	quartered

Brush the fish fillets with a little oil or butter and sprinkle over smoked paprika. Place on a tray to go under the grill.

Cook the diced bacon or chorizo in a pan until colouring, then add the onions and garlic. Continue cooking until soft. Meanwhile, place the fish under the grill.

Add the chilli, the drained cannellini beans, and tomatoes to the bacon mix. Wilt the spinach in the microwave, squeeze excess water out and add. Alternatively, add raw but cook for a little longer as it will dilute the sauce. Cook until heated through. Squeeze in lemon juice and season to taste. Pour into 4 bowls and top with fish, it should be lightly browned, there is no need to turn the fish whilst grilling.

This works well with chicken instead of fish or sausages. You can replace spinach with cooked kale. The recipe is quite versatile.

Vegans could use vegan bacon or chorizo and top with a slice of roast celeriac.

SMOKED HADDOCK SCOTCH EGGS

"I love these, but, they can be a bit like wrestling a jellyfish if the haddock mix is a bit soft. Well worth the effort though."

Makes 3

300g smoked haddock skinned and boned
1 egg white
1-2 Tbsp double cream

Chopped chives and black pepper
3 large eggs
Flour / egg / breadcrumbs for coating

If the eggs are coming from the fridge, cover with hot water, bring to a boil and simmer for 3 minutes. Immediately plunge into ice cold water. If the eggs are at room temperature, drop into boiling water for 5 minutes and cool.

Pat the haddock dry on kitchen paper and chop into cubes. Place in food processor and pulse with the egg white and cream to a puree but with some texture still. Tip into a bowl and season with chives and pepper.

Put seasoned flour in a bowl, a beaten egg in another and breadcrumbs in 1/3.

Carefully peel the boiled eggs and toss in the flour. Divide the fish mix in 3 and with a little oil or flour on your hands flatten each into a disk and shape it around the eggs. Toss each in flour again, then the beaten egg and then the breadcrumbs.

Heat a fryer or saucepan (no more than 1/3 full) with oil until a cube of bread dropped in bubbles and floats.

Drop the eggs carefully into the oil and cook until golden brown and hot through.

SMOKED HADDOCK (OR EGGS)
FLORENTINE

"To be fair, this hardly qualifies as a recipe as it is so easy. But it is one of my favourite go-to lunches or supper dishes from store cupboard and freezer ingredients that are knocked up in minutes!"

Portion 1

3-4 blocks of frozen leaf spinach or 100g fresh leaf, wilted
150-200g smoked haddock frozen or fresh (or 2 eggs)
2 Tbsp double cream
50g grated cheese: cheddar, smoked gruyere, anything that needs using
Salt and pepper.

If using frozen spinach and frozen haddock, defrost in a microwave. Butter individual baking dishes and spread well-squeezed-out spinach over the bottom. Season. Lay fish fillet on top, or if using eggs make 2 hollows and break them in. Drizzle all over with the cream and sprinkle evenly with cheese.
Bake in preheated oven at 200°C until the sauce is golden and bubbling and the fish is cooked. If using eggs, keep an eye on them to just set, otherwise, you will have bullets.
Substitutes - salmon, white fish, chicken breast (lightly cooked first), eggs, etc

Spanish Cod

"This healthy little dish is carb-free and great served with some green beans or salad."

Serves 2

2 x 200g portions cod or other
   firm white fish
4 slices serrano ham
1 small onion, thinly sliced
1 garlic clove, finely chopped
1 vegetable stock cube
100ml white wine or water
3 roasted peppers from a jar, sliced
   (or roast a fresh one)
1 tin chopped tomatoes
1 Tbsp smoked paprika
Salt and pepper
A squeeze of lemon
A splash of olive oil

Season the fish with salt, pepper and lemon juice and wrap each fish fillet in 2 slices of serrano ham.

Heat a splash of olive oil in a small saucepan and add the sliced onion. Cook gently until softening and then add the garlic. Continue to cook until the garlic is colouring then add the paprika. Stir and add the peppers, stock cube, wine or water and tomatoes. Season and cook over low heat until the sauce is reduced and thickened. Tip the sauce into an earthenware dish and place the fish on top. Cook in the oven at 220°C until the fish is cooked and the ham browned around the edges.

Moroccan Fish with Chickpea Tabbouleh

"I used some lovely trout for this but it works well with salmon or any white fish."

Serves 4

4 x 150-200g chunky portions of fish
1 tin chickpeas
150g bulgur wheat
1 fish stock cube
6 spring onions, sliced
1 red pepper, finely chopped
2 small red chilli tomatoes, chopped
2 Tbsp harissa paste
2 cloves garlic, crushed
2 tsp ras el hanout (or more harissa paste)
1 large lemon, zested
Bunch coriander, chopped
Greek yoghurt
Olive oil

Spread the harissa paste over the fish fillets and drizzle with olive oil.

Weigh the bulgur wheat into a bowl and add the stock cube. Just cover with boiling water and leave to swell to double the size.

Preheat the oven to 200°C and cook the fish. While it is cooking, heat some olive oil in a frying pan. Drain the chickpeas well and add. Cook until beginning to brown then add the spring onions, garlic and chopped red pepper. Add the ras el hanout spice mix or some harissa. Cook for a minute and then add the tomatoes and the soaked bulgur wheat. Squeeze in the lemon and add the zest. Cook until heated through and add the coriander. Divide into 4 bowls and top with the fish. Top with some yoghurt and sprinkle with more spring onion or coriander to garnish.

Moqueca

Brazilian fish stew

I had this for lunch, and it's great. Light, full of veg and you can eat it with rice or flatbread to mop up the juices."

Serves 2

250-300g firm white fish-I used hake
1-2 limes
1 small brown onion, chopped small
2 cloves garlic, crushed
1 small carrot, finely diced
1/2 a red pepper, diced small
Olive oil
1 Tbsp tomato puree
1 Tbsp paprika
1 tsp cumin seeds
6-8 slices jalapeño peppers, chopped
250ml water with 1 stock cube (fish or vegetable)
1/2 tin coconut milk
8-10 cherry tomatoes, quartered
1-2 tsp brown sugar
Chopped coriander

Chop the fish into large chunks and squeeze the juice of 1/2 a lime over. Season well with salt and pepper.

In a deep frying pan heat a good splash of olive oil. Add the onion, carrot and garlic and cook until onion is softening. Add the pepper and continue cooking for about 5 minutes until slightly browned. Add the spices and the jalapeño peppers, tomato puree, stock cube, water and season well. Bring to a boil and simmer gently until the carrot is soft, adding a little more water if necessary. You want the liquid to reduce a bit before you add the coconut milk.

Add the cherry tomatoes, sugar and coconut milk, bring to a boil and add the fish with its marinade. Simmer for about 5 minutes until fish is just cooked. Add the other 1/2 of lime juice and taste. It may need more lime or sugar, it should be sharp but with a sweetness too.

Serve in bowls with chopped coriander.

Mediterranean Fish Stew

"I'm feeling a little lockdown stuffed at the moment! So here is something fairly light and very healthy."

Serves 2-3

1 small onion, diced
1 stick of celery, diced
2 cloves of garlic, crushed
4 to 6 small new potatoes quartered
  (optional)
1/2 tsp of fennel seeds
1 tsp smoked paprika
1/2 small red chilli
2 bay leaves and a sprig of thyme

2 anchovies, chopped (optional)
200ml white wine
400ml vegetable or fish stock
1/2 tin chopped tomatoes
Grated zest of 1/2 a lemon
500g mixed fish, cut into large cubes
(I used cod, salmon and large prawns)
Handful chopped parsley

In a medium pan, melt a small glug of olive oil and add onions and celery. Allow to soften and add garlic, potatoes, fennel seeds, smoked paprika, chilli, bay leaves and anchovy, if using. Cook for a couple more minutes and then add wine, stock and tomatoes. Turn down and simmer until celery, potato and onion are soft and flavours developed.

At this point, you could freeze this base for another time or chill if making in advance. (I would leave out the potatoes if freezing.)

Bring back to a simmer and add the assorted fish. Put a lid on and cook for around 5 minutes until the fish is just cooked. Sprinkle over the chopped parsley and serve with rouille if desired.

You can make this with mussels, calamari, any white fish, prawns etc. It works well with a frozen seafood mix.

Thai Prawn and Fish Burger

THAI PRAWN AND FISH BURGER

"Another burger, but this is great for summer. Ideally, you need a food processor, but you could chop the fish very finely. If using frozen fish and prawns, defrost and pat well with kitchen paper to get rid of excess moisture. You could use salmon and probably crab as alternatives."

Serves 2

200g white fish fillet, skin removed & diced
200g raw shelled prawns
2 spring onions, chopped
1 tsp Thai red curry paste

1 tsp finely grated lemon zest
Chopped coriander
Salt and pepper
Oil to fry

Buns, mayo, tomato, lettuce and dill pickles to serve.

Place the spring onions in a food processor and chop till fine. Add the lemon zest, Thai paste, white fish and 1/2 the prawns. Pulse to chop but not too finely then add the remaining prawns and pulse again to roughly chop but leave some chunks. Season and divide in 2. Roll into balls then flatten into patties.

Fry the patties until deeply golden on each side and cooked through. Layer in buns with mayo, lettuce, tomatoes and dill pickle.

Mackerel in Oats with Gooseberry Sauce

2 large mackerel fillets
Porridge oats
1 egg, beaten
Seasoned flour
180g gooseberries
Caster sugar
Knob of butter

"My gooseberries are at an end, so I wanted to use the last handful. Herring in oatmeal is a classic, as is mackerel and gooseberry sauce, so this is a mash-up! I only had jumbo oats so I put them through a coffee grinder. Normal porridge oats are good."

Serves 2

Put the gooseberries in a small saucepan with a tiny splash of water and add about 50g of sugar and a knob of butter. Cook gently until soft and mash roughly. Taste and add more sugar if necessary, it should be sweet but with a sharp edge to counteract the oiliness of the fish.

Trim the fish of any odd fins and check for obvious bones. Skin, if desired. I don't bother, it's easy to remove once cooked if you don't like it. Dip the fillets in the flour, then the beaten egg, and the oats pressing to get an even coating.

Heat a dash of vegetable oil and a knob of butter in a frying pan and when sizzling, add the fish flesh-side down, skin-side up and cook until golden. Turn and repeat.

Serve with the warm gooseberry sauce and spring or summer vegetables.

FISH WITH SAUCE VIERGE

"You can make this with any white fish - cod, haddock, hake, sea bass etc or even salmon. I used sea bream and being greedy, I used 2 fillers just for me as they were quite small...that's my excuse anyway. Traditionally made with olive oil, I made it with butter as I love a butter sauce."

Serves 2

2 medium fillets of white fish
Seasoned flour
1 large banana shallot, finely chopped

100ml white wine
8-10 cherry tomatoes, quartered or smaller
50g butter, diced or 60ml good olive oil
Fresh Green herbs (I used dill, parsley and chives)
Salt and black pepper

Dust the fish fillets with seasoned flour. In a good non-stick frying pan add a little oil and pan fry the fillets until light golden brown and just cooked. Keep warm whilst you make the sauce.

Wipe out the pan with a little kitchen paper and add a little more oil. You need all the ingredients chopped and ready to use. Add the chopped shallots and cook over medium heat until softening, then add the wine. Continue to cook until it has reduced by 1/2. Add the tomatoes and herbs and just warm through, then add the butter or oil. Turn the heat to high to quickly melt the butter or heat the oil, stirring rapidly to emulsify the sauce.

Pour over the fish and serve.

Cod with Chorizo, Pepper,
and Wild Garlic Ragout

"I used peppers from a jar but you can use fresh peppers, just braise them for a little longer when adding."

Serves 2

2 cod fillets
1/2 jar roasted peppers, sliced
1/2 chorizo ring, diced
10-12 cherry tomatoes

2-3 spring onions, sliced
Salt and pepper
A glug of red wine or water
6-8 wild garlic leaves

In a medium frying pan, cook the chorizo with a tiny splash of oil until just colouring. Add the spring onions and peppers and continue cooking until softened. Add the tomatoes and wine or water and braise until the vegetables are softened and the liquid is slightly reduced. Add the wild garlic and season.
Season the fish with salt and pepper and place on top of the ragout. If your frying pan isn't ovenproof, transfer to an ovenproof dish. Bake in the oven at 180°C until the fish is just cooked.
Serve with more chopped wild garlic.

THAI LIME AND COCONUT
CHICKEN SKEWER

"Light and succulent, these make a nice light supper or lunch with coconut rice or salad."

Serves 2

2 chicken breasts
Zest and juice of a lime
125ml coconut milk
2 Tbsp light soy sauce
2 Tbsp light brown sugar
1 tsp ground cumin

1 tsp ground coriander
1/2 tsp curry powder
1tsp ginger puree
1/2 tsp garlic puree
Chopped coriander
Lime wedges

Cut the chicken into 6-8 chunks per breast. Mix all the other ingredients in a large bowl and add the chicken. Marinate for 3-4 hours or overnight.
Skewer the meat onto 2 skewers and place under a high grill. Turn the chicken occasionally and brush with the remaining marinade as its cooking. When browning and charring around the edges, check that it is cooked in the middle and then serve with coconut rice, flatbread or salad with chopped fresh coriander and lime wedges.

Spring Chicken and Vegetable Pot
with Wild Garlic Pesto

SPRING CHICKEN AND VEGETABLE POT
WITH WILD GARLIC PESTO

"Light, healthy, delicious, and very easy to do. To make the wild garlic pesto refer to the Creamy Onion Soup recipe."

Serves 4

1 medium chicken	About 2 Tbsp plain flour
A large knob of butter	600g (or so) assorted green veg
1 onion	(e.g. green beans, asparagus,
1 large carrot	tenderstem broccoli, peas, broad
2 sticks celery	beans etc)
1 chicken stock cube or jelly	1 tin borlotti beans
1 large leek	150g orzo pasta

Place the chicken in a large ovenproof casserole, rub with a little butter and season well with salt and pepper. Roast for about 30 to 45 minutes at 170°C till just lightly colouring. Chop the onion, carrot and celery into large chunks and put them around the chicken. Add the stock cube, cover with a lid or foil and cook for another hour until the chicken and vegetables are soft and cooked. Remove the chicken from the pot and set aside. Cut or pull into portions when cool enough to handle.

Strain the liquid from the pot into a bowl and discard the vegetables. Put the liquid in a saucepan and reduce it to about a litre. Wash the pot and return to the stove and melt a good knob of butter in it. Slice the leek fairly thinly and cook in the butter until softened. Add the flour and cook for a minute, then add the reduced liquid. Stir well as you bring it to a boil, it wants to be like a thin soup. Add the green vegetables, orzo pasta and borlotti beans. Stir well. Lay the chicken back on top and return to the oven for about 20 minutes until the vegetables are just tender.

Serve in bowls with a good dollop of wild garlic and walnut pesto, or basil pesto.

NORTH AFRICAN CHICKEN
USE HALLOUMI FOR VEGGIE OPTION

"This is a bit of a cheat which I do often for lunch. It uses pouches of cooked grains which you can also get in various flavours. It's very versatile and you can add loads of veg to make it super healthy. Green veg like beans, broccoli, or sugar snap peas need blanching briefly in boiling water

Serves 4

2 sachets cooked mixed grains
1 tin chickpeas
3-4 spring onions
2 tsp ras el hanout seasoning
Assorted veg (I used diced tomatoes and blanched tenderstem broccoli, chopped)
Salt and pepper, chopped coriander

3-4 chicken breasts
1 good Tbsp harissa paste
Juice of a lemon
Dash of olive oil

Mix chicken breasts, harissa paste, lemon juice and oil well and leave to marinate for 1 hour or so. If using green veg, blanch briefly.

Heat a frying pan and add the chicken breasts. Cook over medium heat until browning on the outside and just cooked in middle. Keep warm.

In the same pan, with all the juices, add the sachets of grains and break them up with a fork. Season with the ras el hanout and salt and pepper, then toss around for a few minutes until hot. Add all your vegetables, spring onions and coriander, and continue to stir together until warmed through. Tip into a large shallow dish, and top with sliced chicken breast.

You can make a Mediterranean version by using sun-dried tomato paste in place of harissa, omit the ras el hanout and replace coriander with basil or oregano. Drizzle with balsamic glaze at the end.

Other vegetable ideas - mangetout, green beans, broccoli (blanched first), mushrooms, fennel, courgettes (fry in a pan after the chicken before adding grains), spinach (add at the end and wilt).

Mediterranean Chicken Burgers

500g chicken or turkey mince
2 spring onions, finely chopped
Zest of 1 lemon
4-6 sun-dried tomatoes, chopped
75g feta cheese, crumbled
(optional)
Salt, pepper, dried oregano

"A great low-fat burger, good for a barbecue. Full of zingy flavours."

Makes 3 large or 4 small patties

Mix all the ingredients apart from the feta in a bowl until well combined, then carefully mix in the feta. Shape into to 3 large or 4 smaller patties and pan-fry until golden brown and cooked through.
Serve in a bun with your choice of garnishes - salad leaves, spinach, tomato, avocado, dill pickle, and also either mayonnaise, harissa yoghurt, sour cream....

CHICKEN BASQUAELLA

"I've always liked Delia Smith's Chicken Basque but traditionally it would not have rice in it. It's more of a paella, so this is my take (and I do use rice). Let's call it Basquaella! This easily serves 6 but you may want to increase chicken depending on people's appetites."

Serves 4-6

CHICKEN BASQUAELLA

150g spicy chorizo, split in 1/2 and cut into chunks
1 medium chicken, jointed (free range is good) or 8 chicken thighs
1 large or 2 small red peppers, sliced
1 large onion, sliced
2 garlic cloves, finely chopped or garlic puree
20-30g black olives (kalamata are good)
6-8 sun-dried tomatoes, chopped
10 cherry tomatoes, halved
1 Tbsp tomato puree
150ml white wine
300ml or so chicken stock
5-6 sprigs of thyme
Zest of 1/2 orange
300g paella rice

If using a whole chicken, either joint it yourself or ask your butcher to split it into 8 portions.

Heat a splash of olive oil into a large shallow casserole and add the chorizo. Cook until browning around the edges. Remove the chorizo to a bowl and place the chicken portions skin down in the remaining oil. Cook till browned, turning occasionally. Remove to a bowl.

Add the peppers and onion to the pan and cook until softened. Add garlic, stir around for a minute or so then add rice. Stir around again for a minute. Add tomato puree, olives, cherry tomatoes, orange zest, thyme and chorizo. Add the wine and stock. Place the chicken pieces on top and season well.

Cover with a lid and cook in a medium oven at 160-170°C until the chicken and rice are cooked. Add a little more stock or wine if it starts to dry out.

If using a whole chicken, you can brown the wings and carcass in the oven. Then add water and simmer for an hour or so and use the stock.

CHICKEN AND CHORIZO RAISED PICNIC PIE

"In anticipation of warm picnic weather, I thought I would make a picnic pie. Normally I would mince pork belly and bacon, but this is a quick version. I decided to try using chorizo sausage instead of bacon just for a change."

Serves 10

CHICKEN AND CHORIZO RAISED PICNIC PIE

800g pork sausage meat

1 spicy chorizo ring, skinned or skinned

cooking chorizo

4-6 chicken thighs, skinned and boned

Chopped fresh herbs of choice

Salt and pepper

575g plain flour

200g lard

220ml water

1 egg

300ml chicken stock

6 leaves gelatine

In a saucepan, bring the water and lard to a boil. Pour onto the flour in a large bowl and season with salt and pepper. Mix well and knead lightly into a smooth-ish ball. Cover and leave to cool slightly.

Chop the chorizo as finely as possible or pulse it in a food processor. Add to the sausage meat in a bowl with a choice of herbs and seasoning.

Take 2/3 of the pastry; it should be lukewarm and still malleable. Roll into a circle to line a 22cm loose-bottomed deep tin. Push and shape the pastry up the sides to just above the rim. Divide the sausage meat into 2 and press one 1/2 into the bottom of the tin as evenly as possible. Lay the chicken thighs in an even layer on top and season. Press the remaining sausage meat across the top, again, as evenly as possible.

Roll the remaining 1/3 of the pastry into a circle just big enough to cover the top. Beat the egg and brush around the pastry rim and lay the circle on top. Seal and trim the edges. You may have enough trimmings to make some leaf decorations. Brush with egg wash to glaze. Make a hole in the top.

Bake at 200°C for 20 minutes and then turn down to 160°C and cook for a further 2 hours.

Put the gelatine in a bowl of cold water to soften. Heat the stock and add the squeezed-out gelatine. Cool. When the pie is completely cold, use a funnel or spoon to pour gelatine slowly into the hole of the pie. Beware, if you have any cracks, it will pour out.

Asian Pulled Beef Bao Buns

with Asian Slaw

"This is a long recipe but quite easy to do. It just has rather a lot of ingredients. Most supermarkets now sell bao buns, but it works quite well in a burger bun or brioche bun."

Makes 10-12 bao buns

ASIAN PULLED BEEF BAO BUNS

WITH ASIAN SLAW

BEEF

700g-1kg braising steak (I used skirt)
80ml soy sauce (preferably light soy)
1 Tbsp grated ginger or puree
1 tsp grated or pureed garlic
1 tsp five-spice powder
2 star anise
1 Tbsp sesame oil
1 Tbsp fish sauce
1/2 tsp chilli flakes
1 onion, chopped
50g brown sugar
Bao Buns

Put the beef in a casserole or oven-proof saucepan. Add all the other ingredients (except the buns) with 500ml water. Bring to a boil. Cook in a low oven, 160°C for about 2 hours until beef tender and pulls apart easily. Remove the beef and remove and discard star anise. If the stock is too thin, boil over high heat until it is reduced and slightly syrupy. Pour back over beef.

SLAW

1 x 500g bag stir fry vegetable
3 Tbsp vegetable oil
1 Tbsp sesame oil
80ml rice wine vinegar
or white wine vinegar
2 Tbsp honey
2 Tbsp light soy sauce
2 garlic cloves, grated
1 Tbsp gated or puree ginger

In a small bowl, mix all the slaw ingredients together and pour over the vegetables. If the stir fry mix is very coarse, you may want to chop a little smaller. Serve immediately or if you like your veg a little softened, mix an hour or two before serving. Add peanuts just before serving, if using.

OPTIONAL

Chilli flakes
Sesame seeds
Roasted peanuts

Smoked Chicken

Courgette and Sherry Linguini

"This is a delicious and creamy dish. It came about because I visited a local smokery and farm shop, and I also got the first 2 baby courgettes from my plant."

Serves 2

160g linguine
A good knob of butter
1 smoked chicken breast, cut into strips and skin removed
3-4 baby courgettes, chopped
2 small banana shallots, finely sliced
2 garlic cloves, finely chopped

125g mascarpone
125ml amontillado or dry sherry
Salt and pepper
Juice of 1/2 lemon
Splash of cream
Grated parmesan

Cook the linguine according to the instructions on the packet.

Whilst cooking the linguine, melt the butter in a frying pan and add the sliced shallots, garlic and courgettes. Stir around on fairly high heat for 2-3 minutes until just starting to colour. Add the sherry, cook for a moment and then add the mascarpone. Stir well to combine to a smooth sauce. Add the lemon juice, the chicken strips and a little cream to give a rich sauce. Season with salt and pepper.

When the linguine are cooked, drain and add to the sauce. Stir well and divide between two bowls.

Top with grated parmesan.

Moroccan Spiced Beef Flatbread

"I made the flatbreads but they are fairly widely available, and there are lots of recipes online. Uses 4 flatbreads about 18cm in diameter."

Serves 4

400g steak (rump, or bavette is good but bavette needs to only be cooked rare)

MARINADE
3 Tbsp red wine vinegar
1 good tsp garlic granules
1 tsp ground cumin
2 tsp ground coriander
1/2 tsp ground cinnamon
1/2 tsp ground ginger
1/2 tsp ground black pepper
2 Tbsp runny honey
2 Tbsp olive oil
Salt and pepper
1 tin chickpeas, drained
1 shallot or small onion, finely chopped
1 clove garlic, minced
1/2 a lemon squeezed
Chopped coriander
Yoghurt, mint, coriander

Mix all the ingredients for the marinade together in a large bowl and add the steaks. Leave to marinate for minimum 30 minutes, preferably 1 hour or so.

In a non-stick frying pan heat a little oil. Drain the steaks well but keep the marinade. Flash-fry the steak on high heat very briefly to how you like it, then keep warm. Add a little more oil to the pan and add the onions and garlic. Cook gently until softened, then add the chickpeas, remaining marinade and lemon juice. Add a little water or wine if necessary so there is a little juice. Season well.

Warm the flatbreads.

Slice the steak, and tip any juices from it into the chickpeas.

Divide the chickpeas between the flatbreads and top with the steak. Mix chopped mint and coriander with yoghurt and drizzle over. Garnish with chopped coriander.

Beef Suya

Nigerian Street Food

"This recipe is all about the beef. I have done it as skewers but you could marinade and cook whole steaks. If doing skewers. serve with flatbreads and salad."

Serves 4

600-800g rump or sirloin steak
1 Tbsp garlic puree
1 Tbsp ginger puree
1/2 beef stock cube
2 Tbsp oil
80g dry roast peanuts
1 Tbsp smoked paprika
1 Tbsp garlic salt
1 Tbsp onion powder
1 tsp chilli flakes
1 tsp ground ginger
Good pinch of ground cinnamon
Salt and ground black pepper
Red pepper
Large onion
Lime wedges

Dice the beef into large chunks. In a bowl dilute the stock cube in a couple of tsp boiling water. Add the garlic and ginger purees and the oil. Mix well, then add the beef. Mix well. Grind the peanuts in a food processor or coffee grinder as finely as possible. Mix with all the other dry ingredients and a good amount of salt and pepper. Mix into the beef and leave to marinate for as long as possible or overnight.
Cut red pepper and onions into large squares and thread onto skewers alternately with the beef.
Heat the grill to max or a griddle plate. Brush the skewers with a little more oil and grill for 12-14 minutes, turning frequently to ensure they are charred and cooked evenly.
Serve with lime wedges for squeezing over.

Marinated BBQ Bavette

"With the weather getting warmer I'm beginning to think of barbecue. Using bavette steak is super quick, pretty cheap and very juicy. Morrisons sell them or ask your butcher. The most important thing to remember is you must not cook it more than medium as it will go like shoe leather, and cut across the grain when serving. I turned mine into a steak, mushroom, and onion ciabatta......and it was yum. Would work well as a steak salad."

Serves 2 as snack in baguette or ciabatta, or 1 greedy person like me!

1/2 tsp smoked paprika
1 1/2 Tbsp runny honey
Juice of 1/2 a lemon
Good pinch of oregano
Black pepper

100-150g piece of bavette
2 Tbsp light soy sauce
2 Tbsp olive oil
1 tsp minced garlic
1 tsp minced ginger

Mix all the marinade ingredients together in a shallow bowl. Trim the steak of any sinews. Put steak in the marinade and leave for a minimum of one hour.
Drain the steak and either bbq or fry in a hot pan for about 1 -2 minutes max on each side depending on thickness. Do not overcook and always slice across the grain of the meat when serving.

BBQ Pulled Pork and BBQ Sauce

"I've just cooked 20 kilos of this for our street party on Saturday but this recipe is for a smaller number! Making it is really quick but the cooking is low and slow......"

Serves 8-12

"For anyone making the pulled pork who wants to make their own BBQ sauce, here is the recipe I use. It will keep in the fridge for a week or two as it is made with store cupboard ingredients."

BBQ PULLED PORK
2 tsp smoked paprika
2 tsp ground cumin
1/2 tsp garlic salt
2-3 tsp dark brown sugar
1 tsp salt
Black pepper
330ml (1 small bottle) cider
2 - 2.5 kilos boneless shoulder of pork
(ideally skinless)
300ml good BBQ sauce
Burger baps

SAUCE
300ml tomato ketchup
5 Tbsp white wine or cider vinegar
8 Tbsp dark brown sugar or a mix of honey and dark brown sugar
2 Tbsp vegetable oil
1 Tbsp Worcestershire sauce
1/2 tsp English mustard
2 tsp smoked paprika
1/2 tsp ground black pepper

Mix the dry ingredients together and rub into the pork, getting into all the crevices.
Place in a roasting tin and cover with foil and cook at 150°C. After an hour pour over the cider and cover again. Cook for 4-6 hours, or until it will pull apart really easily. Drain any excess liquid but keep enough for it to be moist. Remove any skin and excess fat. Shred the pork with 2 forks and mix in the BBQ sauce.
Serve in burger baps with coleslaw and salad.

Mix all together in a saucepan and bring to a simmer. Cook for 5 minutes and then use or decant into a jar and keep in fridge.
You could add a couple of tablespoons of bourbon or scotch if you like.

Greek Lamb
with Homemade Flatbread

"This is seriously easy and delicious, and the flatbreads are pretty simple and foolproof. Really, give these a go, fabulous for a summer lunch."

Serves 4

FLATBREAD
200g plain flour
200g Greek yoghurt
1 tsp baking powder
Salt and pepper

Mix all the flatbread ingredients together in a bowl until smooth. Leave to rest for 1 hour. Divide into 4 pieces, roll into balls and roll out as thinly as possible to about 21-23cm in diameter. The thinner, the better for big bubbles and air pockets. It will try to stick so don't be afraid to use extra flour. Heat a large frying pan and add a small amount of butter just to cover the surface. Cook each bread on medium heat turning once as it bubbles up until evenly coloured.

LAMB
800g-1kg neck of lamb
2 lemons
2-3 large garlic cloves
1/2 tsp dried oregano
A splash of olive oil
Salt and black pepper
Flat leaf parsley, chopped

Cut the lamb into large chunks. Zest the lemons. Mix the lamb, juice from the lemons, oil, oregano, salt and pepper in a bowl. Either tip into a cast iron casserole pot with a lid, or line the baking tray with a large sheet of foil and cooking parchment, tip in, pulling upsides and sealing at the top. Bake for 3 hours at 150°C.

When the lamb is cooked, add the lemon zest and parsley. Warm the flatbreads briefly in the oven and serve with Greek yoghurt mixed with fresh mint and grated garlic, and Greek salad (tomatoes, cucumber, red onions, black olives and feta).

Za'atar Lamb
with Orange and Date Salad Pittas

"There are two ways to cook the lamb for this: either long and slow for a joint or quickly pan-seared for leg steaks or loin. Great for summer fresh eating or a barbecue."

Serves 6

Za'atar Lamb
with Orange and Date Salad Pittas

MARINADE
Grated zest and juice of an orange
2 Tbsp za'atar spice
1 Tbsp sumac
2-3 Tbsp olive oil
Salt and pepper

Mix the marinade ingredients together and rub all over the lamb. If using the leg or shoulder, you could stab it all over to help it marinade.
Leave for 2-3 hours or overnight.

SALAD
2 oranges, segmented
150g stoned dates, chopped
2 banana shallots
  or small red onion, sliced
1 green chilli, seeded and thinly sliced
Rocket, lambs' lettuce or other baby salad leaves
3 Tbsp pomegranate molasses
2 Tbsp white wine vinegar
125ml olive oil
Pitta Breads

LAMB
Small shoulder for 4-6 lamb steaks

If slow cooking, put the joint on a roasting tin, cover with foil and cook for 3 hours or so at about 160°C until tender and shreddable. Drizzle in 1-2 Tbsp pomegranate molasses and toss through the lamb. If necessary, you can splash in a little wine or water to moisten it.

For steaks: pan fry or barbecue until just cooked. Remove and allow to relax, and then cut into slices and drizzle with 1-2 Tbsp pomegranate molasses.

Mix the orange segments, dates, onion, and chilli together. Mix olive oil, vinegar, 2 Tbsp pomegranate molasses together and mix through. Add the leaves and season well.

Toast pitta bread or on barbecue and stuff with the lamb and salad.

Good with tabbouleh salad.

Greek Lamb Kofta

Greek Lamb Kofta

"I did these with a Greek salad and tahini yoghurt dip."

Serves 4

500g minced lamb
2 tsp ground cumin
2 tsp ground coriander
2 tsp paprika
1/2-1 tsp cinnamon
1 tsp red chilli flakes
1/2 a large onion, grated
2 garlic cloves, grated
1 1/2 tsp salt
Ground black pepper
A small bunch fresh coriander, chopped
Oil to brush

Put all the ingredients into a bowl and mix really well. If desired, you can add a handful of fresh breadcrumbs.

Divide into 4 and shape into long sausages onto skewers. If using bamboo skewers, soak them in water first. Leave the koftas for 1 hour or so in the fridge to relax and develop flavour.

When ready to cook, heat a good cast iron or heavy non-stick griddle, or barbecue. When hot, add the kofta and cook, turning frequently. Turn down the heat and continue to cook until cooked through. If unsure, pop in the oven for 5 minutes or so, but don't overdo as they will go dry.

GREEK SALAD
1/2 a cucumber, diced
200g assorted tomatoes, diced
1/2-1 red or brown onion diced
100g feta cheese, diced
4 Tbsp good olive oil
2 Tbsp lemon juice or white wine vinegar
1 tsp dried oregano
2-3 sprigs of fresh mint, chopped
Good pinch of sugar
Salt and pepper

TAHINI YOGHURT SAUCE
Mix 1/3 tahini to 2/3 thick Greek yoghurt. Add a good squeeze of lemon juice, salt and pepper.

Mix well and leave to marinate in the fridge or at least an hour before serving.

Mushroom and Halloumi Burger

"This recipe serves 2 people although I have been known to use 2 mushrooms for a Burger when I'm really hungry! Easy to make vegetarian, although I used a few chorizo slices I had in the fridge and just popped them on the same tray as the mushrooms halfway through cooking. You can also substitute the halloumi with mozzarella, Stilton or cheddar. Just layer cheese on top of the mushrooms near the end of cooking time."

Makes 2

25g butter, softened
1/2 tsp smoked paprika
1/2 clove garlic, minced or crushed
1 tsp Worcestershire sauce
Salt pepper
2 large portobello mushrooms
4-6 slices of halloumi cheese
2 brioche buns
Mayonnaise
Little gem leaves
Grilled bacon, chorizo slices, avocado slices etc

Mix the paprika, garlic, Worcestershire sauce, salt and pepper into the softened butter and spread all over the top and bottom of the mushrooms. If you like, you can marinate the halloumi in chilli, oil and thyme.

Put the mushrooms on a tray in a preheated oven at 200°C for around 10-15 minutes or until the mushrooms are cooked and browning.

Meanwhile, grill the bacon or chorizo, if using. When the mushrooms are nearly ready, pan-fry the halloumi.

Split buns and toast if desired. Spread mayo on the base, and top with lettuce, bacon etc, mushroom and halloumi. Enjoy!

Minty Lamb Meatballs
with Tahini Sauce

"This is a bit of a fusion dish, Middle Eastern, Turkish and Cypriot. Great as part of a meze, or a light summer lunch."

Serves 6 as part of meze

450g minced lamb	A good squeeze of lemon
2 Tbsp harissa paste	2 garlic cloves, crushed & preferably roasted
Chopped fresh mint	Pomegranate seeds
Salt and black pepper	Toasted pine nuts
2 Tbsp tahini paste	Chopped fresh coriander
4 -6 Tbsp Greek yoghurt	Drizzle of pomegranate molasses

In a bowl mix the lamb, harissa paste, chopped mint, salt and pepper, until well combined. Divide into 24 and roll into small balls. Fry in a little oil on fairly high heat to just brown all over and tip into a baking tin. You may need to fry in two batches. You can do this in advance and pop it into a hot oven for 10 minutes just before serving.

Beat the tahini, yoghurt, lemon and garlic together. Season.

Put the lamb balls in the oven and cook for around 5-10 minutes until cooked through. Tip into a dish with any juices, drizzle with the tahini yoghurt and sprinkle with pine nuts, pomegranate seeds, and coriander. Drizzle with pomegranate molasses and serve with warm flatbreads.

Spinach, Sun-dried Tomato
and Parmesan Quiche

"Quiche has had very bad press over the years, but this is not a wussy quiche!! It's creamy, not watery, rich and yummy. This one is vegetarian but, of course, you can use bacon and onions for a traditional quiche Lorraine. You could make it smaller: just use 4 eggs for every pint of cream."

Serves 10-12

1 x 500g pack shortcrust pastry
  (or a ready-made shortcrust flan base)
200g fresh spinach, wilted and well squeezed
120g sun-dried tomatoes, chopped
150g parmesan cheese, grated
6 eggs
800ml double cream
Salt and pepper

Roll the pastry as thinly as possible to line a 30cm loose-based flan tin. Line with baking parchment and add baking beans or dried pulses. Allow to rest for about an hour before baking at 220°C for 10-15 minutes until the pastry is cooked and lightly coloured. Remove the parchment and beans and return to the oven for 5 minutes.

Chop the spinach and spread it over the base. Sprinkle over the tomatoes and cheese. In a large bowl, whisk the eggs and cream together and season well. Pour over the filling and return to the oven. Reduce the temperature to 160°C and cook for a further 30-40 minutes until the filling is golden all over and just set, but still a little wobbly in the middle. Allow to cool before cutting.

Spring/Summer Vegetables with
Potato Parmesan Dumplings

"My little veg patch is throwing up baby carrots, courgettes and beans but you could use whatever your favourite veg are.
Hopefully, you will have started making your own stock from your roast chicken bones or veg trimmings and peelings. If not, you can buy fresh liquid stock or use stock pot jellies. Light dumplings with healthy tasty veg."

Serves 2

750ml good quality chicken or veg stock
100ml white wine
Fresh herbs of choice
500-600g assorted baby veg
1 large floury potato (about 350g)
1 egg
3-4 Tbsp self-raising Flour
30g parmesan, finely grated
Salt and black pepper
A good splash of cream (optional)

Bake the potato for about 1 hour until soft and fluffy in middle. You can speed this up by microwaving it for 3-4 minutes until it's squealing and then bake it for around 30 minutes.

Scoop out the middle and mash well. Allow to cool and then add the egg, salt and pepper, parmesan and flour. Mix well but lightly, it should be soft but not too sticky. Add a little more flour, if necessary. Shape with floured hand into 6-8 balls and leave aside.

Heat the stock with the wine and fresh herbs. Add the vegetables in order of cooking time; carrots will take longer than courgettes etc.

Remove all the veg and keep warm. Add the dumplings and cook for about 6-8 minutes until they float, then remove and add to the vegetables to keep warm.

Reduce the stock over a high heat to about 1/2 and then add cream if using. I like to add baby spinach and allow it to wilt. Pour over the vegetables and dumplings. Serve.

GNUDI

"I'm having fun making gnudi, a softer lighter version of gnocchi using ricotta cheese instead of potato. They are delicious! I served them with 2 different sauces: cherry tomato, basil and pine nuts, and bacon, portobello mushrooms and spinach."

Serves 2

250g ricotta	35g plain flour	Salt and pepper
50g finely grated parmesan	1/2 large egg	Semolina

Drain the ricotta in a sieve to remove excess liquid. Tip into a bowl and add the parmesan, flour and egg. Mix well and season well.

Sprinkle the work surface well with semolina and tip out the ricotta mix. It will be quite soft. Split into 2 pieces and gently roll each into a log about the diameter of a 2-pence coin. Cut into around 10 pieces for each log and coat well in the semolina. Place on a tray sprinkled with semolina, leaving space between them. Chill until ready to cook.

Make your sauce (see below). Boil a pan of water large enough to take all the gnudi with plenty of space and drop them in. They are ready when they float, though I give them an extra 30 seconds or so to be sure. Scoop out into your sauce along with a splash of the cooking water. Toss around and serve with plenty of grated parmesan.

SAUCE OPTION 1: Bacon, portobello mushrooms and spinach.
Fry 6-8 rashers-worth of chopped streaky bacon until beginning to brown lightly, add 1 large diced portobello mushroom and continue to cook on fairly high heat to brown the bacon and fry the mushroom. Add a couple handfuls of fresh spinach and allow to wilt. Add a good knob of butter, allow to melt and then add a good squeeze of lemon. Now you can add the gnudi.

SAUCE OPTION 2: Tomato, basil and pine nut sauce.
Toast a handful of pine nuts in a dry pan. Soften 2 sliced spring onions in a good glug of olive oil. Add about 10-12 halved cherry tomatoes and cook to just softening. Add a small handful of chopped basil and soften. Add a splash of balsamic vinegar and then add the pine nuts. Now you can add the gnudi.

Buckwheat Crêpes/Breton Galette

"Buckwheat doesn't contain gluten so it is possible to make these gluten-free, if you replace plain flour with extra Buckwheat or gluten-free flour. They will be more fragile so take care flipping them."

Makes 6 portions

120g Buckwheat flour
60g plain flour
1 tsp salt
7g instant yeast
1 large egg
325ml buttermilk
   or milk and yoghurt mixed
225ml warm water
Vegetable oil (for frying)

Possible fillings: cooked spinach, fried garlic mushrooms, cheese, eggs, cooked bacon, ham, cooked chicken, kidney or haricot beans, tomatoes, sauteed leeks, and cooked kale.
I used spinach, mushrooms, gruyere and egg.
In a large bowl, mix the flour, salt and yeast. Make a well in the centre and add the egg, water and buttermilk or milk mix and whisk well to make sure it is lump-free. Leave in a warm place to rise for around an hour. It should be bubbly but won't have grown much in size.
A good non-stick frying pan is pretty essential for these, about 25-30cm. Add a little oil and whisk the batter one more time. Add just enough batter to the pan and swirl around quickly, as thinly as possible. Cook on medium heat and then loosen from pan and flip once pale golden brown. Cook the other side and make another five, stacking them on a plate. Stuff each pancake with your choice of filling and put it on a well-oiled baking tray. If using an egg, leave a hole in the middle when stuffing and drop the egg in when on the baking tray. Pop them in a hot oven until they are warmed through, the cheese has melted, and the egg is just cooked.

GOAT'S CHEESE TARTS

"I've made two different goat's cheese tarts, a caramelised fennel and apple, and fig and red onion. They both use the same base."

Serves 6

GOATS CHEESE TARTS

FOR ONE TART:
125g plain flour
80g butter
1 egg + 1 yolk
200ml double cream
120g soft goats' cheese
Salt and pepper

1 bulb of fennel, thinly sliced
30g butter
1 tsp caster sugar
1 small eating apple, peeled, cored and diced
30g walnuts, chopped

1 large red onion, finely sliced
30g butter
1 tsp caster sugar
4 figs, quartered
1 Tbsp balsamic vinegar
Runny honey

To make the pastry, rub the butter into the flour until it resembles fine breadcrumbs. Bring together with a teaspoon or two of cold water until it forms a smooth ball. Allow to rest for 30 minutes, then roll as thinly as possible and use to line an 21cm flan case. You could, of course, use ready-rolled shortcrust pastry.

For the fennel and apple: melt the butter in a small frying pan and cook the fennel over medium heat until softened and beginning to go golden. Add the apple and the caster sugar and continue to cook until deep golden.

For the fig and caramelised onion: melt the butter and cook over medium heat until softened and beginning to colour. Add the caster sugar and the balsamic vinegar and continue to cook until lightly browned.

Allow the pastry to rest for 30 minutes before baking blind in an oven at 200°C for around 10 minutes until pale golden.

Remove the baking beans and add either the fennel mixture or the onion mixture. Slice or crumble the goats' cheese evenly over the tart. Lay the figs over the onion mixture.

Whisk together the eggs and cream and season with salt and pepper. Pour into the tart and bake at 160°C until just set, sprinkling the chopped walnuts over the fennel tart halfway through the cooking time.

Drizzle the fig tart with a little honey.

COURGETTE, PEA AND MINT PASTA

'I love this pasta! The mint makes it light and summery, and I often add some diced cooked bacon or ham!"

Serves 2

2 small courgettes, coarsely grated
50g frozen peas
180g pasta of choice
Generous knob of butter
1 tsp finely chopped fresh mint

1/2 vegetable stock cube
About 70-80ml white wine
100ml double cream
Freshly grated parmesan to serve
Salt and black pepper

Put the courgettes in a bowl and sprinkle them fairly well with salt. Leave for 30 minutes or more and then put in clean tea towel or muslin and squeeze out as much water as possible.

Put a large saucepan on to boil. When boiling, add the pasta and stir well. Turn down and leave to cook according to instructions on the packet.

Melt the butter in a medium frying pan and add the courgettes. Stir around for a minute or two until softening slightly, then add the peas. Add the wine and stock cube and boil vigorously for a minute or two to reduce the wine. Add the mint and cream and ham (if using), and simmer until thickened slightly. Try not to overboil as the veg will lose their vibrant colour.

Drain the pasta and add to the sauce. Mix well and serve with plenty of grated parmesan.

STUFFED COURGETTES

"Just when you thought you had enough courgette recipes, I had to make this as a very simple light lunch. I found these courgettes on a farmers market and used a quick cheat to create."

Serves 2

2 round courgettes
1 pack ready-cooked Mediterranean flavour grains
1/2 pack feta cheese
A few sprigs of basil

Olive oil
Splash of white wine
Salt and pepper

Cut the stem end of the courgettes and keep to put back on top. With a spoon, scoop out the seeds but don't take too much flesh.

Put the grains in a bowl and crumble in the feta. Chop the basil and add. Lightly season the inside of the courgettes and then stuff tightly with the grains. Put the stem back on top.

Place in a small tin and add a splash of wine to each. Brush with olive oil and bake at 180°C for 30-40 minutes until just soft and hot in middle. You can test with a skewer. You could serve it with some extra tomato sauce.

Mushroom Ragout
with Fried Polenta

"Hopefully you have made the soft polenta and have some leftover which has now set. You could add fried diced chorizo, bacon pancetta or spinach."

Serves 2

2 portions firm polenta, sliced
10g dried porcini mushrooms
200g portobello mushrooms, sliced
1 medium shallot, sliced
1 large garlic clove, crushed
1 tsp flour

8-10 cherry tomatoes, halved
Splash of dry sherry or white wine
Chopped fresh basil
A knob of butter
Olive oil
Salt and pepper

Put the porcini mushrooms in a small bowl and just cover them with boiling water.

Toss the sliced polenta in a little raw polenta and fry in olive oil until just crisp and lightly browned. Keep warm.

In a frying pan, add a good knob of butter and cook the shallot on medium heat until softened. Add the garlic and the portobello mushrooms and continue to cook until browning, adding a little more butter if necessary. Add the flour and stir for a minute or so. Add the tomatoes, soaked porcini with soaking liquid, sherry, salt and pepper to taste and bubble until lightly thickened. When ready to serve, stir in the basil and serve over the fried polenta.

SOFT POLENTA

"To be honest, I was never a lover of polenta. Maybe I didn't have a good one before, but now I really quite like it. I have used instant polenta. Normally polenta needs stirring for 30-40 minutes and whilst there is a difference in taste and texture, the time-saving makes it a good option. Allowed to go cold and set, you can use it for fried polenta or polenta chips. I used roasted garlic. It's worth roasting 2 or 3 whole bulbs at a time and storing them in the fridge covered with olive oil."

Serves 4-6

125g instant polenta
4 cups water
1 chicken stock pot
1/2 a bulb of roasted garlic

50g butter
75g parmesan, grated
Salt and pepper

Put the water and the stock pot in a saucepan and bring to a boil. Turn off the heat and whisk in the instant polenta. It will thicken after a minute or so. Mash or puree the roast garlic with the butter and stir through the polenta with the parmesan cheese. Season to taste and serve immediately or pour into an oiled dish and chill until set to use for fried polenta.

GREEK LEMON ROAST POTATOES

"I used salad potatoes. They hold their shape and soak up all the flavour."

Serves 6

750g Charlotte potatoes (or similar)
2 Tbsp lemon juice
3-4 Tbsp olive oil
2 cloves of garlic, minced or grated
1 tsp dried oregano
1 tsp dijon mustard
Ground black pepper
Pinch of salt
100ml chicken or vegetable stock

In a bowl mix lemon juice, oil, garlic, mustard, oregano, salt and pepper. Mix well and add the potatoes, halved lengthways.

Heat oven to 200°C. Tip the potatoes and juice into a roasting tin and roast for about 20 minutes. Add the stock and mix together. Continue roasting until the liquid is absorbed and the potatoes are golden brown.

Desserts
and
Cakes

Karythopitta

"This lovely moist cake is full of nuts, but light and delicious. I was short of walnuts but made up the difference with pistachios which makes me think it would work really well with all pistachios."

Serves 8-10

KARYTHOPITTA

170g unsalted butter, melted
45g dried breadcrumbs
170g ground walnuts
150g caster sugar
2 tsp baking powder
1.5 tsp ground cinnamon
zest of 1 lemon, finely grated
5 eggs

SYRUP
Juice of 1 lemon
75ml water
140g caster sugar
2 Tbsp brandy
2 Tbsp honey

Preheat the oven to 190°C. Line the base of a 24cm loose-bottomed cake tin with non-stick baking parchment and grease the sides.

First, make the syrup so that it is completely cool by the time the cake is done. Put the lemon juice, water, sugar and brandy into a saucepan and stir over a moderate heat. Bring up to a boil and simmer for 5 minutes. Stir in the honey and leave to cool.

To make the cake, melt the butter and cool until lukewarm. Mix the breadcrumbs with the finely ground walnuts, salt, sugar, baking powder, cinnamon, and lemon zest in a mixing bowl. Pour the lukewarm butter into the centre of the dry ingredients and break in the eggs. Beat until thoroughly mixed and pour into the prepared tin. Bake for 40-50 minutes until the cake feels firm to the touch. Test by plunging a skewer into the centre. If it comes out clean, the cake is done. When the cake comes out of the oven, pierce it all over with a skewer. Pour the cold syrup, little by little, over the hot cake, spooning any syrup that oozes out the centre of the cake every now and then, until it has all been absorbed.

Serve with Greek yoghurt.

APRICOT, MARZIPAN,
AND PISTACHIO SLICE

"Got some lovely fresh apricots from the farmers market yesterday so I made this super quick super easy apricot slice. It's almost just a put-together-and-bake dessert that tastes great."

Makes 2 slices - 8 portions

1 pack ready-rolled puff pastry
12-14 large apricots
1 pack (450g) natural marzipan
Chopped pistachios
Runny honey

Preheat oven to 200°C.

Unroll the pastry and cut in 1/2 lengthways and place it on a large baking tray with space between. Cut a rim around the edge of each about 1cm wide but don't cut right through. This will help to make a border.

Cut 2/3 of the marzipan into thin slices (about 16) and lay down the centre. Halve the apricots and remove the stones. Lay evenly on top of the marzipan cut-side down. Grate the remaining marzipan and sprinkle over the apricots, avoiding the edges.

Bake for around 15-20 minutes until golden brown, then turn the oven down to 160°C. Sprinkle with the chopped pistachios and drizzle with runny honey. Bake for a further 5 minutes or so to lightly toast the pistachios.

Serve with cream or ice cream.

QUICK AND SIMPLE ICE CREAM

"As temperatures reach 40°C, I thought I would share this really easy ice cream recipe. Here I made it coconut-flavoured but have previously also made coffee, strawberry and chocolate chip ice cream: pretty much any flavour. As you can see from the photo, I couldn't resist tucking in!"

Makes about 1 litre

50g desiccated coconut	600ml double cream
A little milk	1 tin condensed milk
	Vanilla paste/ extract

Put the coconut in a small bowl and just cover it with milk. Leave to stand for an hour or so until softened and plumping up. You can speed this up by heating it in the microwave for 30 seconds to a minute and then leaving it to cool.

Whisk the double cream until just lightly thickening. Do not over-whisk! You want it soft and fluffy. Add the condensed milk and whisk again to combine and until light and fluffy. Fold in the vanilla and drained coconut. Pour into a plastic pot and freeze. You will need to remove it from the freezer for a few minutes before serving to allow it to soften slightly.

To make coffee flavour: add a tablespoon of coffee essence or really strong sweetened coffee. For strawberry: fold in 1 or 2 tablespoons strawberry coulis.

SOUR CREAM AND REDCURRANT SLICE

"Between my dog and the birds my redcurrant crop was somewhat diminished, but I managed to get enough to make this. You could substitute all or part of the fruit with raspberries, blackcurrants, diced apples etc."

Makes 8-10 slices

300-350g Redcurrants

BASE
140g softened butter
160g caster sugar
1 egg
1 tsp mixed spice
200ml soured cream
200g self-raising flour

CRUMB TOP
150g self-raising flour
115g butter
50g rolled oats
100g caster sugar

Line the base of a shallow baking tin approx 28cm x 22cm with baking parchment. Preheat oven to 180°C

First, make the crumble. Rub the butter into the other crumble ingredients until well-mixed and knobbly.

Beat the butter and sugar together with a whisk or wooden spoon until pale, light and fluffy. Beat in the egg. Add the spice, sour cream and flour and spread over the base of the tin. Sprinkle the fruit evenly over the mixture. (You could sprinkle the fruit with a little extra sugar if it is particularly sharp.)

Evenly sprinkle the crumble mix over the fruit and bake for about an hour until firm in the middle. Dust well with icing sugar or caster sugar.

SUMMER PUDDING

"It's called summer pudding, but this works equally well with frozen red fruit and cheers up a grey winter day. Have to say that this is my daughter's favourite pudding so it is perfect any time of year."

Serves 6-8

1.25kg mixed summer fruit (raspberry, strawberry, red currants, blackberry etc.)
180g caster sugar
8 -10 slices of good white bread, day or more old

Lightly oil a 1-litre pudding bowl and line it with cling film.

Cut the crusts off the slices of bread and cut 6 slices diagonally lengthways to make 2 pieces slightly triangular. Cut one slice into a round to cover the base of the bowl and then tightly fit the triangular slices narrow-point down around the sides.

Put the fruit and sugar into a saucepan and heat until the juices are beginning to run, and the sugar is dissolved. Try not to boil it as the fruit will go soggy.

With a slotted spoon, spoon 1/2 of the fruit into the bread-lined bowl, draining slightly so it is not too wet. Lay a slice of trimmed bread over and then add the remaining fruit, draining slightly again. Keep the remaining juice. Lay another layer of bread on top to cover the fruit completely and then cover it with cling film. Find a saucer or disc of some sort that is just smaller than the top of the pudding and place it on top, weighing it down with something heavy to press the pudding.

Refrigerate the pudding overnight then turn out onto a plate. Spoon the remaining juice over to cover any white bits.

Serve with cream.

INSTANT BANANA ICE CREAM

"Got some bananas going a bit soft? This is a fab way of using them up."

1 dessert

For every banana you need:
2 Tbsp double cream
1 Tbsp Greek yoghurt
1 Tbsp honey or maple syrup

You could use coconut milk in place of the cream and yoghurt if you want to make it vegan.

Peel and chop the bananas and put them in the freezer in a plastic bag or tub. Leave until really solid, preferably overnight.

Place bananas in a food processor and add the rest of the ingredients. Pulse until all blended and smooth. It can be eaten immediately as a soft scoop. For a firmer dessert, put back in the freezer for a while to set.
Serve with chopped pecan, grated chocolate, wafers or whatever you fancy.

TIRAMISU

"This is a really simple dessert, and you can make it even easier if you cheat and buy ready-made fresh custard. In this recipe, I make the custard which is really quite simple. I cheat by buying a sponge flan case, you know, the sort your gran used to fill with tinned fruit."

Serves 8

400ml milk
150ml double cream
1 tsp vanilla paste
1 level Tbsp cornflour
50g caster sugar
4 egg yolks

2 cartons mascarpone cheese
1 large sponge flan case
100ml strong coffee, lightly sweetened
100ml marsala or brandy
50g dark chocolate, grated

First, make the custard. Warm the milk and cream to almost boiling. Meanwhile beat the sugar, egg yolks, vanilla and cornflour together. Pour the hot milk and cream slowly onto the egg mixture, whisking all the time. Return the mixture to the saucepan and bring it gently back to a boil. Cook for an extra minute, stirring all the time to prevent catching on the bottom. Pour into a bowl and allow to cool. (You can sprinkle a little caster sugar over the top to prevent a skin)

Trim the sponge to fit on the base of your dish. Keep the trimmings. Mix the coffee and marsala together and drizzle 2/3 over the base. Sprinkle over 1/2 of the grated chocolate.

Fold the mascarpone into the cooled custard and pour 1/2 over the base. Top with the sponge trimmings and drizzle with the remaining coffee mixture. Top with remaining custard mix and smooth.

Top with remaining grated chocolate.

Rhubarb Crumble Cheesecake Tart

"I found new seasons forced rhubarb in the supermarket, so this is a mash-up of 3 different desserts using what I had in the cupboard and fridge. You could add stem ginger to the rhubarb or nuts to the crumble."

Serves 8

RHUBARB CRUMBLE CHEESECAKE TART

RHUBARB

400g rhubarb
A little butter
Caster sugar

RHUBARB

Chop the rhubarb into 2.5-5cm chunks. Melt a little butter in a roasting tin, toss the rhubarb in to get coated with butter. Sprinkle well with caster sugar and roast in a 180°C oven until just soft, 10-15 minutes.

PASTRY

200g plain flour
100g butter or clover
60g caster sugar
1 large egg yolk

PASTRY

In a food processor (or you can rub in by hand) rub the butter into the flour. Add the sugar, the egg yolk and a very tiny splash of water and pulse until just combined. Wrap in cling film and rest for 30 minutes. Roll out to fit a 25cm flan tin with overhang, line with baking parchment and fill with baking beans or dried pulses, and bake at 200°C for 15 minutes until just colouring.

CHEESECAKE

100g cream cheese
200ml double cream
1 whole egg plus one yolk
40g caster sugar
1 tsp vanilla paste or extract

CHEESECAKE

Beat together all the cheesecake ingredients. Remove the baking parchment from the flan and gently spread rhubarb over the base. Pour the cheesecake mixture over. Reduce the oven to 160°C and bake for 15 minutes.

CRUMBLE

40g oats, porridge or jumbo
80g self-raising flour
50g butter or clover
30g caster sugar

CRUMBLE

Rub the crumble mixture together quite well so that it is slightly lumpy rather than dusty. Place on a baking sheet and cook along with the tart for 10-15 minutes until lightly golden. Crumble it up a bit and sprinkle over the tart. Continue to bake until the cheesecake is just set.

Tarta De Queso

San Sabastian Cheesecake

"I ate this whilst in San Sebastian. It is rich but light, as it doesn't have a base and just 5 ingredients. It's often called burnt cheesecake and it should be darker in colour than mine came out so I have adjusted the cooking in the recipe."

Serves 4

540g cream cheese
   (I used 3 standard tubs of Philadelphia)
175g caster sugar

3 large eggs
300ml double cream
20g plain flour

Preheat the oven to its max, about 240°C. Line a 20cm round deep cake tin with greased baking parchment. You can either do this neatly by cutting the parchment and lining the base and sides or the traditional way of pushing the whole sheet in which gives rustic-looking sides.

Beat the cream cheese and sugar together with a hand whisk or beat by hand. Add the eggs one at a time, beating between each. Add the cream and flour and beat lightly until all is incorporated and there are no lumps of flour. Tip into the lined tin.

Put into a very hot oven and turn down to 200°C. Bake for about 40 minutes, the cheesecake should still be wobbly in the middle but quite brown. Allow to cool completely before cutting. Serve at room temperature, with fruit or coulis.

You could add lemon zest or vanilla if you wanted but it's not traditional.

ROASTED SWEET CHILLI PINEAPPLE

"This is great with coconut ice cream."

Serves 4-6

1 medium pineapple (must be ripe)
100g light brown sugar
 2 Tbsp pomegranate molasses

1 Tbsp balsamic vinegar
1/2 tsp chilli flakes
Good pinch of salt

Top, tail and peel the pineapple. Put the remaining ingredients in a small saucepan with 1 Tbsp water and heat until melted.
Put the pineapple in a small roasting pan and pour over the sauce. Roast the pineapple at 160°C for 30-40 minutes, turning every so often and basting.
Remove the pineapple and heat to reduce the thick sauce and then pour over the pineapple to serve. Serve whole or in slices with cream or ice cream.

Raspberry and Pistachio Frangipane Tart

Raspberry and Pistachio Frangipane Tart

"Based on a French frangipane tart this uses Pistachios instead of almonds."

Serves 8

1 block puff pastry (or ready-rolled if not confident rolling yourself)
I jar good-quality raspberry jam
180g butter or Clover, softened
180g caster sugar
3 large eggs
150g pistachios, ground in processor
50g self-raising flour
150g fresh raspberries

Roll the pastry as thinly as possible to line a deep flan tin (25cm in diameter, 25cm deep). Trim excess pastry and spread the jam evenly over the base.

In a large bowl whisk the butter and sugar together until light, creamy and fluffy. Beat in the eggs one at a time and then fold in the ground pistachios and flour. Spread evenly over the jam. Sprinkle the raspberries evenly over the cake mix.

Bake at 220°C for 10-15 minutes. Then turn the oven down to 180°C and continue cooking until the top is golden brown and the middle is just set. Allow to cool and dust with icing sugar. Serve with more fresh raspberries and cream

Profiteroles / Choux Ring

PROFITEROLES / CHOUX RING

"A lot of people have problems with choux pastry, but it is fairly easy to make, providing you follow some important rules."

Serves 8

300ml or 1/2 pint water
100g/4 oz salted butter
120g/5oz plain flour
4 large eggs
570ml or 1 pint double cream

SAUCE
200g dark chocolate
300ml double cream
2 Tbsp soft brown sugar

In a large saucepan put the water and diced butter and bring to a boil. You need to dice the butter so that it is melted by the time the water boils. The water must boil, otherwise the flour will not be cooked when it is added.
Remove from the heat. Add the flour and beat well until totally mixed with no lumps, it may help to use an electric hand whisk. The mixture should come away from the sides of the pan.
Allow to cool for about 5 minutes. Add the eggs one at a time, beating really well between each one. The mixture should drop slowly from the spoon and be soft; not runny, but not too stiff either.
Pipe or spoon out onto parchment-lined trays with good space between them as they should double in size. For the ring: pipe out onto parchment into a ring about 25cm in diameter.
Bake at 220°C for 20-25 minutes until golden brown and crisp. If they are too pale, they will deflate when removed from the oven. The ring will take longer, and you may need to turn the oven down a bit to prevent over-browning.
Cool on racks. Fill with whipped double cream when cold, do not overwork the cream, it should hold soft peaks.

SAUCE
To serve, drizzle with chocolate sauce. Warm the double cream and sugar until the sugar has dissolved. Remove from heat and add the chocolate. Whisk until all is incorporated into a smooth sauce.

PETIT POT AU CHOCOLAT

"Very rich!"

Makes 6
ramekins

150ml double cream
150ml milk
150g dark chocolate, broken into cubes
75g brown sugar

20g butter
1 whole egg + 2 yolks

Whisk the sugar and eggs together in a bowl until pale and creamy.

Pour the milk and cream in a small saucepan and heat until not quite boiling. Take off the heat and whisk the chocolate in until melted and lump-free. Pour the chocolate mix onto the egg mix and whisk until fully amalgamated. You can add a shot of brandy or another liqueur if desired.

Split between the ramekins. Put the ramekins in a small roasting tin and pour boiling water around them.

Place in a low oven, about 150°C, and bake for about 20 minutes until just set but still a little wobbly. Do not allow it to boil otherwise the texture will be grainy! Cool and serve.

PINK GRAPEFRUIT POSSET

"I know I'm always saying certain recipes are dead simple and quick. Well, in this case it's really true: 5 minutes to make, but about 2 hrs to chill."

Serves 4

570ml double cream
140g caster sugar
1 pink grapefruit
1 small lemon

Zest and juice the lemon and grapefruit. Put the cream, zest and sugar in a saucepan and bring to a simmer. Continue to simmer gently for a couple of minutes.
Take off the heat and add the citrus juices. Stir well and strain into glasses. Chill until set.

How easy is that?!

RASPBERRY AND MANGO PAVLOVA

5 large egg whites
283g caster sugar
1 Tbsp lemon juice
1 Tbsp cornflour
1 tsp vanilla paste
400ml double cream
300g fresh raspberries
1 ripe mango

"I'm sure many of you have made Pavlova with various degrees of success. I hope you find this recipe successful."

Serves 8-10

In a very clean bowl (stand or mixer), whisk the egg whites until almost stiff, then add the lemon juice and continue whisking until very stiff peaks are formed. Add the caster sugar, heaped tablespoons at a time with the whisk running at full speed. When all the sugar is incorporated, turn the whisk to a slow or medium speed and add the vanilla and cornflour. , Whisk briefly to incorporate, do not overmix. Line a baking tray with baking parchment and spread the meringue into a deep disc about 21-25cm in diameter.

Bake at 100°C for 1 hour until set and firm when pressed but still pale in colour.

Slide the meringue on the parchment and onto a cooling rack.

When cold, lightly whisk the cream to soft peaks. Do not over whisk, it will thicken as you spread it over the pavlova.

Peel, stone and dice the mango and decorate the pavlova with this and the raspberries. If the mango is a bit under-ripe, you can simmer it for a couple of minutes in a splash of orange juice and some caster sugar to soften it. Cool before using. Other soft fruits work well.

HOT RHUBARB SOUFFLÉ

"You can make this with other fruits: raspberries, gooseberries, mango, etc. With rhubarb you don't need sieve after thickening. You may need less sugar, depending on your fruit."

Serves 6

500g rhubarb, chopped
280g sugar
50g cornflour
1 tsp vanilla paste
Red food colouring (optional)
3 large egg whites
Butter and caster sugar for lining ramekins

Put the rhubarb and 250g of the sugar in a saucepan with the merest splash of water just to start the cooking process and bring to a simmer. Cook gently until the rhubarb is completely soft. Mix the cornflour with very little water, just enough to mix and add to the fruit a little at a time over low heat, stirring constantly until the mixture thickens. You may not need it all. It should be a thick puree. Whizz with a hand blender and cool. Add food colouring, if using. If using raspberries, gooseberries (or other seeded fruit), pass through a sieve to remove pips.

When ready to cook, generously butter 6 ramekins and coat with caster sugar.

In a clean bowl, whisk the egg whites to stiff peaks and then add the rest of the sugar (30g) and whisk a little more till glossy.

Gently fold 1/3 of the egg white through the fruit until soft and then fold in the remaining whites. Spoon into the ramekins right to the top. Tap gently to make sure there are no gaps. Smooth off the top, and run your thumb around the rim to make a small gap. Place onto a baking sheet and bake in the preheated oven at 200°C for around 10 minutes until well risen and cooked through. Dust with icing sugar and serve immediately!

GOOSEBERRY CUSTARD STREUSEL CAKE

"A German classic, and a delicious use of gooseberries. It is quite easy to make. The custard in mine is very white as I didn't add egg yolk, but I think it needs it for better colour."

Serves 8-10

CAKE and STREUSEL
400g self-raising flour
200g butter or Clover
200g cater sugar
2 eggs
200g gooseberries, topped and tailed
1 Tbsp caster sugar
1 heaped tsp cornflour or arrowroot

CUSTARD
250ml milk
200ml sour cream
30g cornflour
3 Tbsp caster sugar
1 tsp vanilla paste
1 egg yolk

Whisk together the ingredients for the custard. Pour into a saucepan and bring gently to a boil and cook for a minute until thick.

Toss the gooseberries with the 3 Tbsp caster sugar and cornflour or arrowroot.

Rub the butter or Clover into the flour until evenly rubbed in and knobbly. Add the caster sugar and rub together a bit more until incorporated.

Weigh 300g of the mix and set it aside. To the remaining mix, add 1 egg and the egg white leftover from the custard.

Butter a deep 23-25cm quiche tin or springform loose-bottomed tin and press the cake mix into the bottom and slightly up the sides with damp fingers. Tip over the gooseberries and spread out. Pour the custard over the gooseberries and sprinkle crumble over the top.

Bake in a preheated oven at 200°C for 20-30 minutes until golden, then turn down to 150°C for another 20 to 30 minutes until the gooseberries are soft and cake cooked through.

Gooseberry and Elderflower Fool

350g fresh gooseberries
70g caster sugar
3 Tbsp elderflower cordial
180ml double cream
80ml thick Greek yoghurt

"I'm inundated with gooseberries this year so here's the first of, no doubt, many gooseberry recipes. Traditionally, a Fool was made with custard and cream but using Greek yoghurt makes it lighter and quicker. If you prefer the traditional, use the same amount of ready-made custard. Here's a use for the elderflower cordial if you made it."

Makes 4

Put the gooseberries, caster sugar and elderflower cordial in a small saucepan and bring gently to a simmer. Cook until the fruit is soft. Using a hand blender, blend to a puree and, if desired, pass through a sieve to remove seeds but it's a matter of choice. Allow to cool.

Lightly whisk the cream to soft peaks and fold through the yoghurt. Fold in the cooled gooseberries and divide between 4 glasses.

Gluten-Free Churros

with Chocolate Sauce

"My friend is gluten-intolerant but was craving churros, so these are for her."

Serves 4-6

GLUTEN-FREE CHURROS

WITH CHOCOLATE SAUCE

CHOCOLATE SAUCE
300ml double cream
2 Tbsp brown sugar
200g dark chocolate

CHOCOLATE SAUCE
Warm 300ml double cream in a saucepan with 2 Tbsp brown sugar until sugar has dissolved. Remove from heat and add 200g of dark chocolate. Stir until the chocolate is melted and the sauce is smooth and glossy.

CHURROS	150g gluten-free flour
250ml water	1 tsp vanilla paste/extract
50g butter diced	1 egg, beaten
1 Tbsp caster sugar	Oil to fry
A good pinch of salt	Caster sugar and cinnamon mixed

CHURROS
Put the water, butter, sugar, and salt into a medium saucepan and just bring to a boil. Remove from the heat and add the vanilla. Add the flour and beat really hard until smooth with no lumps. Allow to cool slightly for about 5 minutes and then beat in the egg a little at a time until smooth. If it feels too stiff, add a little more egg. It should be stiff, but soft enough to pipe.

When ready to cook, heat oil in a large pan, no more than 1/3 deep. Do not leave! Drop a small piece of bread in, it is hot enough when the bread floats and bubbles.

Tip the churros mix into a piping bag with a star nozzle and pipe into the oil, cutting with scissors as it comes out in short lengths. You will have to do this in batches.

Cook until golden brown on both sides and floating. Drain on some kitchen paper, then mix 1 tsp of cinnamon into a bowl of caster sugar and toss the churros in it. You can warm the churros again in the oven briefly if required. Serve with the warm chocolate sauce.

Buttermilk Panna Cotta

"I love panna cotta, but it can be a bit rich. Using buttermilk gives it a natural sharpness which works well with fresh fruit."

Serves 4

300ml double cream
80g caster sugar
1 tsp vanilla paste/extract
3 sheets gelatine
300ml buttermilk

TOPPING
1 large mango
juice of 1 lemon
1 Tbsp sugar

Put the gelatine sheets in a bowl and cover with cold water.

Warm the double cream, sugar and vanilla in a saucepan until just coming to a boil and the sugar is dissolved. Squeeze out the gelatine sheets and stir through the cream until completely dissolved. Add the buttermilk and mix well. Pour into 4 glasses and chill in the fridge until set. Top with fruit of choice.

I used 1 large mango, peeled and diced, cooked in the juice of a lemon and caster sugar until syrupy.

Chill and top.

Bougatsa with Honey Poached Figs

"This is a light, simple dessert, great for a dinner party. I added the pistachios after I took the photo."

Makes 6-8

FILLING
200ml milk
100ml double cream
1 egg
2 tsp cornflour
2 Tbsp semolina
60ml caster sugar
Vanilla essence/paste

PASTRY
6-8 sheets of filo pastry
melted butter

FIGS
6-8 large figs
2 Tbsp runny honey
Zest and juice of an orange
Pistachios
1/2 tsp ground cinnamon

Put all the filling ingredients into a non-stick saucepan and whisk well to amalgamate. Gently bring to a boil, stirring all the time until thick. Pour into a shallow bowl and sprinkle lightly with caster sugar to prevent a skin from forming.

Brush each sheet of filo pastry with a little butter and cut into squares. Pile 3 squares on top of each other and push gently into muffin tins. Repeat with the rest of the pastry to make 6-8 bougatsa. Split the custard between them, and then push the edges into the middle to enclose. Brush with some more butter and bake at 180°C until golden brown.

Cut a cross on top of each fig and place it in an ovenproof dish just big enough to hold them. Drizzle with the honey, sprinkle with orange zest and squeeze over juice. Sprinkle over the cinnamon and bake with the bougatsa until soft. Toast and chop the pistachios then sprinkle over.

BLUEBERRY AND COCONUT TARTE

"I was short on time, so I used a block of readymade shortcrust pastry, but feel free to make your own!"

Makes 8-10 portions

300-400g shortcrust pastry
2-3 Tbsp jam (optional)
170g softened butter or Clover
170g caster sugar

2 large eggs
110g desiccated coconut
110g self-raising flour
200g fresh or frozen blueberries

Roll the pastry as thinly as possible and use it to line a 25cm flan tin, leaving a slight overlap to allow for shrinkage. You do not need to bake this tart blind before adding the filling!

Spread the jam over the base. Beat the softened butter and caster sugar together until light and creamy. Beat in the eggs one at a time. Add the coconut and flour. Spread evenly over the jam. Sprinkle the blueberries evenly over the top and bake in preheated oven at 200°C for 20 minutes. Turn the oven down to 180°C and continue to cook until the cake is set and cooked in the middle. Trim the excess pastry with a sharp knife and dust with icing sugar.

Whole Orange Polenta
and Almond Cake

"This is a cross between two different recipes. I had 2 blood oranges in the fruit bowl so used them up in this cake - gluten-free!!"

Serves 8

2 oranges (250-275g)
4 large eggs
160g caster sugar
150g ground almonds
50g polenta

100ml veg oil or 100g melted butter
2 tsp baking powder
Syrup
Juice of 1 lemon and 1 orange
40g caster sugar

Put the oranges in a small saucepan just big enough to hold them and cover them with water. Bring to a boil and simmer until very soft, about 30 minutes. Puree in a food processor or with a hand blender.

Grease and baseline a 23-25cm cake tin .

Put the eggs and sugar in a bowl and whisk until thick and airy, and doubled in volume. Whisk in the melted butter or oil briefly, and then fold in the almonds, polenta, baking powder and pureed oranges.

Pour into the tin and bake at 160-170°C until evenly golden and set in the middle. Turn onto a cooling rack.

Put the orange and lemon juices in a small saucepan and add sugar. Bring to a boil and simmer until syrupy. Pour over cake. Serve with crème fraiche or clotted cream.

LIME AND COCONUT DRIZZLE CAKE

LIME AND COCONUT DRIZZLE CAKE

"Light, citrusy and summery."

Serves 8-10

250g softened butter
250g caster sugar
250g beaten egg (4-5 eggs)
120g desiccated coconut
150g self-rasing flour
Zest of 2 limes

SYRUP
Juice of 3 limes
80-100g sugar

ICING
Zest of 1 lime
100g butter, softened
200g icing sugar

Grease a loaf tin approximately 25 x 12cm and dust with flour.

Whisk together the butter and caster sugar until very pale and fluffy. Add the egg a little at a time, whisking after each addition. Add the lime zest and self-raising flour and whisk briefly to incorporate. Pour into the loaf tin and bake in a moderate oven, about 170°C for around 40 minutes or until golden brown and a skewer inserted into the middle comes out clean with no wet mixture on it. Turn out and allow to cool.

Meanwhile, put the juice and sugar in a small saucepan and bring to a boil. Simmer for a couple of minutes and turn off.

When the cake is cool, pierce the top and bottom all over with a skewer and drizzle the syrup all over.

Whisk together the softened butter, icing sugar and lime zest until light and fluffy and spread or pipe over the top of the cake. Decorate with lime slices or coconut.

Baked Peaches with Almonds
with Marsala Cream

"I picked up white peaches by mistake, I think it's nicer with yellow-fleshed peaches or nectarines. Perfect light dessert for the summer and very easy."

Serves 2

PEACHES
2 ripe peaches or nectarines
60g ground almonds
30g caster sugar
1/2 egg approximately, beaten
15g butter, softened or melted
1 Tbsp runny honey
1 Tbsp lemon juice
1/4 tsp vanilla paste

MARSALA CREAM
100ml double cream
Splash of marsala
Dash of runny honey

Whisk together the double cream, marsala and honey together until just thickening.

Halve the peaches and remove the stone. If they are ripe, you should be able to twist the peach to separate and remove.

Put into an ovenproof dish just big enough to hold them. Mix the lemon, honey and vanilla together and spoon over and around them.

Mix together the almonds and sugar, then add just enough egg to bind everything into a thick paste. Add the softened/melted butter and mix well. Divide between the peaches.

Bake at 200°C for around 20 minutes until the peaches are soft and the topping golden.

Serve with marsala cream, ice cream, yoghurt, whatever your preference.

PEACH MELBA UPSIDE DOWN CAKE

"I actually made this with nectarines but either is good. They do need to be ripe though!"

Serves 6-8

CAKE

2 Tbsp melted butter	2 eggs
100g caster sugar	225g self-raising flour
4 peaches or nectarines	1/2 tsp bicarbonate of soda
150g softened butter	1 tsp vanilla paste/extract
150g caster sugar	110g Greek yoghurt

SAUCE

300g raspberries
Caster sugar
1 tsp arrowroot or cornflour

CAKE

Preheat the oven to 160°C. If using a loose-based tin, line it with some baking parchment to prevent leaks. You need a round tin about 21-23cm.

Pour melted butter into the base of the tin and sprinkle evenly with 100g caster sugar. Slice the peaches and lay them in concentric circles in the base.

Beat the butter and sugar together until light and fluffy, beat in the eggs one at a time, then add the remaining cake ingredients, whisk quickly and spoon over the peaches. Spread evenly and bake in the oven for around 1 hour until evenly browned and a skewer pushed into the top of the cake comes out cleanly. Leave to cool well before removing from the tin as there may be some juice in the base.

SAUCE

Put the raspberries and some sugar in a small pan with a couple of tablespoons of water, bring to a boil, simmer until soft and pour through a sieve. Pour back into the pan, mix arrowroot with very little water and add. Bring to a boil to thicken. Then cool.

Serve the cake with raspberry sauce and some Greek yoghurt sweetened with a little sugar and flavoured with some vanilla.

GENOISE SPONGE
WITH RASPBERRIES AND LEMON

"So, just back from holiday, the sun is shining and no doubt the family will be looking to come for lunch. This traditional Gateaux sponge can be made the day before and decorated the next day. There is no raising agent in the cake, it relies on the air that you whisk into the mixture which makes it light and perfect for fresh cream filling."

Serves 8

Genoise Sponge

with Raspberries and Lemon

5 large eggs, at room temperature

145g caster sugar

145g plain flour

70g butter melted

1 tsp vanilla paste

Zest of a large lemon

Caster sugar for drizzle and dusting

The most important thing with this recipe is to get as much air into the mix as possible. This can be done by whisking the eggs and sugar in a bowl over a pan of water that has been boiled and turned off. Or, if you have a stand mixer, put the eggs and sugar in the bowl and let it stand in very warm (but not too hot) water for a few minutes, then whisk. The mixture should become really thick and mousse-like and should triple (or more) in volume. If you lift the whisk, it should leave a ribbon-like trail over the mixture.

Now, sieve the flour over the mixture, add the vanilla and lemon zest. Carefully fold them in with a large metal spoon as gently as possible, trying not to knock out too much air. When 1/2 mixed, add the melted butter and continue to fold, making sure you get down to the bottom of the bowl to mix thoroughly. As soon as you add the butter, it will start to lose volume so mix lightly but well.

Pour into a greased and floured 21cm hinged or loose-bottomed tin and bake at 170°C for around 20-30 minutes until the cake comes away from the sides of the tin and the middle is just set. Cool well.

You can wrap the cake well in cling film and decorate the next day with any fresh fruits, nuts, jam, caramel etc.

300g double cream

300g raspberries

1 jar good quality lemon curd

Juice of a large lemon

FOR RASPBERRY AND LEMON FILLING

Heat the juice of the lemon with a couple of tablespoons caster sugar and bring to a boil. Simmer until syrupy and cool. Divide the cake in 1/2 horizontally and drizzle lemon syrupy over the bottom 1/2. Spread over the lemon curd and cover with the raspberries.

Whisk the cream very lightly until just starting to thicken. It will thicken more as you spread it over the raspberries. Gently place the top on and dust with a caster or icing sugar.

STRAWBERRY POLENTA CAKE

"This is not gluten-free, but it is low in gluten. You could probably replace the flour with equal parts polenta and ground almonds. It makes a light, moist cake with a slightly crunchy crust."

Serves 8

150g strawberries, diced large (keep 4-5 to halve for the top)

170g softened butter + some for tin	2 eggs
170g caster sugar	100g self-raising flour
1 tsp vanilla paste	70g polenta + some for tin
1/2 tsp almond essence	70g ground almonds

Butter a 25cm springform cake tin and dust with polenta.

Beat the butter and caster sugar together until light and fluffy. Beat in the eggs one at a time. Add the vanilla and almond essence, the polenta, ground almonds and flour. Beat together lightly until all is mixed. Stir in the diced strawberries and pile them into a baking tin. Spread out evenly and top with the halved strawberries to decorate. Sprinkle lightly with a little polenta and caster sugar.

Bake at 180°C for around 45 minutes until golden, crusty and cooked in the middle. Serve with clotted cream or ice cream.

Mango Muffins

"I bought a bag of 4 wonky mangoes so needed to come up with some mango recipes. Here's one."

Makes 12

320g plain flour
80g caster sugar
80g dark brown sugar
1 tsp ground cinnamon
2 tsp bicarbonate of soda
1 large mango, peeled and diced
50g sultanas

50g chopped pecans
Juice of a lemon
2 eggs
160ml vegetable oil
Juice of 1/2 a lemon
Icing sugar

Preheat the oven to 180°C. Beat the eggs and oil together. Weigh all the other ingredients into a bowl and add the oil and egg mixture. Mix lightly, but well. Line a muffin tin with muffin cases and fill.
Bake for about 25-30 minutes until golden brown and cooked in the middle.
Allow to cool. Mix the juice of 1/2 a lemon with enough icing sugar to make a thin paste. Drizzle over the muffins and allow to set.

Chocolate Fudge Cake

with Fudge Frosting

"This recipe makes a celebration-size cake that serves 12 to 16, and you need 2 x 25cm cake tins. You could halve the cake recipe and use 2 x 18cm sandwich cake tins for a smaller more teatime-sized cake, but you will need 2/3 the recipe for the frosting. In this photo, I made one and a half times the recipe to give a very large cake for my daughter's colleagues at work."

Actual Recipe (as below) serves 12-14

CHOCOLATE FUDGE CAKE
WITH FUDGE FROSTING

CAKE

350g self-raising flour	4 eggs
4 Tbsp good cocoa powder	300ml vegetable oil
2 tsp bicarbonate of soda	300ml milk
300g caster sugar	4 Tbsp golden syrup

CAKE

Grease and baseline cake the tins with baking parchment. Preheat the oven to 160°C.

Weigh dry ingredients into a bowl and add the remaining cake ingredients. Whisk well until light, smooth and lump-free. Split between the two tins and bake for about 30-40 minutes (less for smaller tins) until a cocktail stick or skewer inserted into the top comes out clean. Turn it out on the cooling rack and allow it to cool completely.

FROSTING

300ml double cream	100g dark brown sugar
200g dark chocolate, chopped	40g butter

FROSTING

Put cream, butter and brown sugar into a saucepan and heat gently until the sugar is melted. Remove from heat and add chocolate. Keep stirring until the chocolate is melted and the frosting is smooth and glossy. Do not overheat once the chocolate is added as it will go grainy and dull.

Put 1/3 of the frosting in a bowl and refrigerate. Leave the other 2/3 at room temperature.

When ready to finish the cake, whisk the refrigerated frosting till pale and fluffy and sandwich the 2 cakes. Ideally, chill the cake at this point.

The other 2/3 of frosting should still be fairly malleable and soft enough to pour over the cake and spread gently over the top and sides. You can warm it very slightly if necessary but be careful, not too much, otherwise it will just pour off the cake.

Chill slightly and decorate with whatever takes your fancy.

OAT AND SULTANA COOKIES

"These are proper cookies: crisp on the outside and a bit chewy in the middle."

Makes around 18 cookies

120g sultanas
150g vegetable oil
200g light brown sugar
1 egg, beaten
1/2 tsp ground cinnamon
1 tsp vanilla paste
140g plain flour
1/2 tsp bicarbonate of soda
300g oats

Put the sultanas into a small bowl and add enough boiling water to just cover them, about 50 to 60ml. Leave to soak for about 20 minutes.

Put sugar and oil into a large bowl and whisk together for a minute. Add the egg and beat again.

When the sultanas are plump and cool, add to the egg mixture with the soaking water. Add all the remaining ingredients and mix until well combined.

Line 2 baking trays with baking parchment and drop dessertspoon of the mix on, leaving space to spread. Flatten slightly. Bake at 180°C for 12-15 minutes until golden brown all over. Leave to cool on the tray for 10 minutes until firm enough to move to a cooling rack. Keep in an airtight tin.

MALTED MILK BISCUITS

"Malted milk biscuits were my favourite as a child. You know, the ones with the cow on them. This is as close as I can get."

Makes 12-14 biscuits

125g unsalted butter
125g caster sugar
1 tsp of good quality vanilla extract
3 Tbsp of golden syrup

1 medium free-range egg
320g plain flour
50g malted milk powder
1tsp bicarbonate of soda

Preheat your oven to 180°C/Fan 160°C.
Line two large baking trays with grease-proof paper. In a large bowl beat together the butter, sugar and vanilla.
Add the syrup and the egg to the mixture and beat. Then add the flour, malted milk powder and bicarbonate of soda and mix thoroughly until it comes together as a ball.
Divide the dough into two equal parts and using a rolling pin, roll the dough until you have the thickness of a pound coin. Use as little flour as possible. You could roll it between 2 sheets of greaseproof paper.
Cut into biscuit-sized rectangles. Use a fluted pastry roll cutter if you have one. Place in the baking tray, and repeat with the remaining dough, Bake for around 10-12 minutes then cool.

Farmer Cheese and Sirniki

Russian Cheese Pancakes

"This is a homemade cheese which is very easy to make and can be used for all sorts of recipes like these pancakes. You can also make the pancakes using strained cottage cheese or quark.
To make the cheese you will need a clean cheesecloth or muslin cloth.

Makes 6-8

FARMER CHEESE AND SIRNIKI
RUSSIAN CHEESE PANCAKES

FARMER CHEESE
Makes about 1-2kg or so.
2.2 ltr whole pasteurised milk
60ml lemon juice (about 2 large lemons)
1 tsp salt

In a large saucepan, heat the milk to the boiling point, stirring frequently to prevent it from burning on the bottom of the pan. When the milk boils, add the lemon juice and stir briefly. It does need to just boil otherwise it may not curdle. Leave to sit for around 15-20 minutes. If you shake the pan, you should see that the milk has separated into curds and whey.
Line a colander with the cheesecloth or muslin and put it over a large bowl. Carefully pour the curds and whey into the cloth and leave to strain. When cool, draw up the sides and squeeze the remaining whey from the curds. Tip the curds into a bowl and season with salt.
The whey is good for making bread or adding to smoothies.

SIRNIKI PANCAKES
Makes 6-8
225g farmer cheese or strained cottage
cheese or quark

1 large egg	80g plain four
1 Tbsp vegetable oil	1 tsp baking powder
3 Tbsp caster sugar	1/2 tsp vanilla paste

Beat all the ingredients together in a bowl to a thick paste. It should be thick enough to drop, in spoonfuls, onto a floured workspace and shape into discs but still soft and a little difficult to handle. If necessary, add a little more flour but not too much as they will get tough.
Heat a non-stick frying pan with a little oil and fry the pancakes on each side to a golden brown. Be careful! They can colour quite quickly, turn the heat down if so, and if necessary, pop into a warm oven for a few minutes to ensure they are cooked through. Serve with fresh fruit, maple syrup, golden syrup, and chocolate....
(I imagine it's possible to make a savoury version, I'll give it a go soon...)

ECCLES CAKES

1 x 500g block puff pastry
600g sultanas, or a mix of dried fruit
100g melted butter
100g dark brown sugar
Zest and juice of a large lemon
1-2 tsp mixed spice
1 egg, beaten
Caster sugar

"An old traditional favourite, I made a big one as I had 1/2 a block of ready-rolled pastry left, but this recipe below will make a batch of 9 cakes. I like mine with just sultanas, but currants are traditional."

Makes 9

Mix the fruit, brown sugar, butter, mixed spice, lemon zest and juice together in a bowl.

Roll the pastry out to a square of about 36 x 36cm. Cut into 9 squares (3x3). Divide the fruit mix between the squares and bring the edges into the middle of each square to seal the fruit in the middle. Gently roll out each cake into a disc, with the join underneath. Place on a baking tray lined with baking parchment and brush with a beaten egg. Score 2-3 cuts in the top and sprinkle with caster sugar. Bake at 220°C for about 15-20 minutes until golden brown.

Allow to cool and dust with icing sugar.

Bread
and
Baking

Pesto and Mozzarella Garlic Bread

"I've still got lots of wild garlic pesto so decided to make pesto bread. Then I got greedy and decided to pimp it up with garlic butter and mozzarella. You could use a jar of shop-bought pesto. I made stuffed balls but it was quite time-consuming so you could roll them out to form a long Swiss roll shape spread them with pesto and coil them into the baking tin."

Serves 4-6

Pesto and Mozzarella Garlic Bread

250g strong bread flour
1 tsp instant yeast
2 Tbsp olive oil
8g salt

Wild garlic pesto
50g softened butter
1 large garlic clove, crushed or grated
Chopped parsley
Salt and pepper
1 ball mozzarella

Mix the flour, yeast, olive oil and salt together and add 150-160ml warm water. Knead well either on the counter or in a food mixer. If kneading on the counter, it should be quite sticky. Don't worry; keep kneading for about 5 minutes. Scrape off your fingers and form into a ball. Wash your hands and then sprinkle a little flour on a surface and knead into a ball. Place in a lightly oiled bowl, cover with cling film and leave to rise for about an hour or until nearly double in size.

Meanwhile, beat the garlic butter ingredients together.

Butter or oil a 20cm sandwich cake tin. Turn out the dough onto a lightly floured surface. Cut it into 10 pieces, shaping each into a disc and put a small amount of pesto in middle, bringing the sides up to form a ball. Place evenly around the tin leaving space to rise. Alternatively, roll into a long thin rectangle, spread with pesto and roll up from the long side and coil into the base of the sandwich tin. Brush with beaten egg or milk and allow to rise to double in size. Bake in a 200°C oven for 15-20 minutes, or untill golden brown and cooked.

Allow the bread to cool when it comes out of the oven, then cut 3-4 times across, but not all the way through. Turn 45 degrees and repeat. Stuff spoonfuls of the garlic butter in the cuts and the sliced mozzarella. Bake again for 5-10 minutes until melted.

CHEESE AND SPRING ONION SCONES

"This is my savoury version of a cream tea. Instead of clotted cream it's cream cheese and Instead of jam, it's chilli jelly."

Makes 8

ACCOMPANIMENTS
Cream cheese
Chilli jelly or jam

SCONES
250g self-raising flour
80g butter
100g cheddar cheese, grated
2 spring onions, chopped
Salt and pepper
120ml milk

OTHER OPTIONS
Smoked cheese
Stilton and walnut,
sun-dried tomatoes
crisped bacon or chorizo
chives
crumbled feta
olives

In a large bowl, rub the butter into the flour until it resembles breadcrumbs. Add the chopped spring onions, cheese, salt and pepper and mix to incorporate. Add the milk, mix lightly into a ball and turn onto the worktop. Knead lightly; it should be a soft dough. Shape and roll out to 2-3cm thickness. Cut with a scone cutter or into squares or triangles. You should get about 8 scones. Sprinkle with extra cheese, if desired.

Bake at 200°C for around 20 minutes until deep golden and cool on a wire rack. Split and serve with cream cheese and chilli jelly.

CHILLI AND CHEESE HOT CROSS BUNS

"Easter is coming! So, as I prefer savoury, I've made this recipe. These are quite mild; you could add extra chilli flakes or powder for more heat..."

Serves 2

625g strong bread flour
455g milk
1 Tbsp caster sugar
2 tsp salt

85g butter
10g instant dried yeast or 20g fresh yeast
3-4 finely chopped fresh chillies
100g grated cheddar
50g grated parmesan
1 Tbsp smoked paprika

Warm the milk and butter to hand temperature. Add the yeast and mix well. In a large bowl or bowl of food mixer mix together the flour, salt, and sugar together. Add the milk mixture, mix well. Either knead in the food mixer or turn out onto the counter. Knead really well until the mixture is smooth and elastic. Add the cheeses, chilli and smoked paprika and knead again until everything is incorporated and even in colour.

Turn into an oiled bowl, cover with cling film and leave to rise for about 2 hours. It will probably be slow as it is an enriched dough. It should rise to about 1/2 as much again.

When risen, turn out onto a floured surface and divide into 12. Roll each portion into a ball and place on a baking sheet with enough space between them to rise well. They should double in size, covered with some oiled cling film.

Beat an egg and brush over buns to glaze.

To make the cross beat together plain flour and water to a paste loose enough to pipe. Make a little piping bag with parchment or put a small nozzle in the piping bag and pipe the crosses.

Bake at 220°C until golden brown and cooked through. You can brush with more egg halfway through for a deeper glaze

Hot Cross Buns

"Not long now till Easter! I know I have already added a chilli and cheese hot cross buns, but I thought a recipe for classic fruit ones would be useful."

Makes 6 but can double easily

250g strong white or wholemeal flour
  (or a combination of both)
120ml milk
1 tsp instant-dried yeast
1/2 tsp mixed spice
1/2 ground cinnamon

50g sultanas
  (or mixed dried fruit)
30g caster sugar
1/2 a beaten egg
20g butter

Put flour, sugar, yeast, spices, fruit and sugar in a large bowl.

Warm the milk with the butter until the butter has melted. Allow to cook to around blood temperature and add the egg. Mix well and pour onto the dry ingredients and mix to a soft dough.

Turn onto the counter and knead for around 5-10 minutes. Do not worry if it is sticky, keep kneading until smooth. Shape the dough off your hands and wash them. Dust the dough with a little flour and shape it into a ball. Place into a lightly oiled bowl and cover with cling film. Leave to rise until doubled in size.

Turn out onto a floured surface and cut into 6 equal portions. Shape each into balls. Place on an oiled baking tray. Cover with some oiled cling film and allow to rise to double size again.

Mix some flour with water to a thick but pipeable paste to make the crosses. Brush buns with some beaten egg and pipe with a cross.

Bake at 200°C for around 20-30 minutes until golden-brown and cooked to the middle. Brush with some melted apricot jam if desired.

FOCACCIA

"If you are new to bread-making, this is a good bread to start with. It doesn't need shaping as it's pretty much free form, but it is quite a soft, wet dough."

Makes 1 loaf

500g strong bread flour
350ml warm water
7g (1 sachet) instant dried yeast
12g salt
2 Tbsp extra virgin olive oil + more for oiling tin and drizzling
Toppings: rosemary, sea salt crystals, olives, sun-dried tomatoes, cherry tomatoes, basil, parmesan, etc

In a large bowl put flour, salt and dried yeast. Mix in warm water and olive oil. Turn onto a clean work surface and knead well. It will be very soft and sticky but keep at it for about 10 minutes. (You can also do this in a stand mixer with a dough hook.)
Scrape into a ball. Use a little flour to remove excess dough from your heads. Shape it into a ball and put it in a bowl covered with cling film. Leave in a warm place until double in size.
Oil a 25x35cm tin quite liberally and gently tip the dough in. Gently push the dough evenly out to the corners. Leave to rise again for about 20-30 minutes. Rub your fingertips with some oil and press into the dough to make dimples.
Top with your choice of flavours and bake in preheated over 220°C for 20 minutes until a pale golden.

Speciality Items
and
Gift Ideas

ELDERFLOWER CORDIAL

"I make this every year from this recipe that I have used for a good 20 years. It's very easy and you can get the citric acid online or from your local chemist. It is necessary as it helps it to keep. It's quite sweet but again necessary for the same reason."

Makes 1 1/2 - 2 ltrs

20 large elderflower heads
  (just opened and creamy white)
1.8kg sugar, granulated or caster
1.2 ltrs water
2 large lemons
75g citric acid

Shake the flower heads to remove any insects still in them. (Don't worry too much as you will be sieving the finished cordial so the odd one won't matter.)

Put the elderflower into a large bowl or bucket. Peel the zest from the lemons and add. Combine the sugar and water into a large saucepan and bring to a boil. Pour over the elderflower and lemon zest. Squeeze the juice from the lemons in and throw in the shells (don't worry about the pips). Add the citric acid and stir everything together. Cover and leave for 24 hours at room temperature.

After 24 hours line a sieve with muslin, or a new J-cloth over a large bowl and pour syrup through.

Decant into clean sterilised bottles. To sterilise: pour boiling water into a bottle and leave for 10 minutes before tipping out.

Serve chilled and diluted with still or sparkling water, or with sparkling wine.

SWEET PICKLED CUCUMBER

2 x 250g boxes of little cucumbers
(you can also use larger ones)
310ml white wine vinegar
125ml water
Scant 1 Tbsp salt
3-4 Tbsp sugar, to taste
Scant Tbsp each: mustard seeds,
coriander seeds and black peppercorns
2 bay leaves
1 banana shallot, finely sliced
2 large garlic clove, sliced

Heat vinegar, water, salt, sugar, mustard seeds, coriander seeds, black peppercorns, garlic and bay leaves together to dissolve sugar and then cool.

Slice the cucumber and shallot and mix well in a bowl. Pour over the vinegar and mix well.

Pack the cucumber and shallot tightly into a sterilised jar and pour over the vinegar mix. Seal tightly and keep in the fridge, which will allow to marinate. Can be eaten after a day or so.

"It must be the time of year, but I'm suddenly into pickling, preserving and chutney-making. This is a quick pickle, designed to use within a month. Great with burgers, smoked fish, Swedish meatballs or in salads."

Makes one large jar, approximately 900g

Index

of

Recipes

STARTERS AND LIGHT BITES

Creamy Onion Soup with Wild Garlic and Walnut Pesto
Fresh Asparagus Soup
Authentic Falafels and Roast Garlic Hummus
Chickpea Flour Crackers Gluten-Free
Muhammara
Savoury Egg Custard or Crustless Quiche
Burrata, Pesto, and Tomato Salad
Griddled Peach, Serrano Ham, Feta, and Walnut Salad
Leftover BBQ Salad with Buttermilk Dressing
Asian Beansprout Salad
Celeriac Remoulade
Chicken, Walnut, and Pomegranate Salad
Tuna Mayo Potato Salad
Panzanella Salad
Courgette and Smoked Salmon Roulade
Prawn and Spinach Aranchini
Thai Salmon Fish Cakes
Thai Spiced Mussels with Irish Soda Bread
Southern Spiced Fish Nuggets
Aubergine and Goat's Cheese Sandwiches
Beetroot Tarte Tatin
Blooming Onion
Char Siu Pork
Chorizo and Goat's Cheese Parcels
Classic Spanish Tortilla

Starters and Light Bites

Gözleme - Spinach and Fetta

Shakshuka

Homemade Potato Gnocchi

Spanakopita

Stuffed Mushrooms

Stuffed Courgette Flowers with Honey

Sticky Chinese Pork Belly

Sweet Potato Fritters with Harissa Yoghurt and Poached Egg (GF-Veg)

Picnic Loaf

Tomato Gruyère Tarts

Spinach and Sun-dried Tomato Cheesecake

Goat's Cheese Mousse with Beetroot and Candied Walnuts

Deep Fried Egg

Coconut Prawns with Mango Mayo

Cheese Beignets

Akoori - Indian Spiced Eggs

Confit Tandoori Chickpeas with Yoghurt Flatbread and Yoghurt Dressing

BBQ Corn with Chilli and Parmesan

Indian-Spiced Cauliflower Fritters

Parmigiana

Main Courses

Salmon Teriyaki

Smokey White Fish and Bean Stew

Smoked Haddock Scotch Eggs

Smoked Haddock (or Eggs) Florentine

Spanish Cod

Moroccan Fish with Chickpea Tabbouleh

Moqueca Brazilian Fish Stew

Mediterranean Fish Stew

Thai Prawn and Fish Burger

Mackerel in Oats with Gooseberry Sauce

Fish with Sauce Vierge

Cod with Chorizo, Petter, and Wild Garlic Ragout

Thai Lime and Coconut Chicken Skewer

Spring Chicken and Vegetable Pot with Wild Garlic Pesto

North African Chicken - Use Halloumi for Veggie Option

Mediterranean Chicken Burgers

Chicken Basquaella

Chicken and Chorizo Raised Picnic Pie

Asian Pulled Beef Bar Buns with Asian Slaw

Smoked Chicken Courgette and Sherry Linguini

Moroccan Spiced Beef Flatbread

Main Courses

Moroccan Spiced Beef Flatbread

Beef Soya - Nigerian Street Food

Marinated BBQ Bavette

BBQ Pulled Pork and BBQ Sauce

Greek Lamb with Homemade Flatbread

Za'atar Lamb with Orange and Date Salad Pittas

Greek Lamb Kofta

Mushroom and Halloumi Burger

Minty Lamb Meatballs with Tahini Sauce

Spinach, Sun-dried Tomato and Parmesan Quiche

Spring/Summer Vegetables with Potato Parmesan Dumplings

Gnudi

Buckwheat Crêpes/Breton Galette

Goat's Cheese Tarts

Courgette, Pea and Mint Pasta

Stuffed Courgettes

Mushroom Ragout with Fried Polenta

Soft Polenta

Greek Lemon Roast Potatoes

DESSERTS AND CAKES

Karythopitta

Apricot, Marzipan, and Pistachio Slice

Quick and Simple Ice Cream

Sour Cream and Redcurrant Slice

Summer Pudding

Instant Banana Ice Cream

Tiramisu

Rhubarb Crumble Cheesecake Tart

Tarta De Queso San Sabastian Cheese

Roasted Sweet Chilli Pineapple

Raspberry and Pistachio Frangipane Tart

Profiteroles/Choux Ring

Petit Pot Au Chocolat

Pink Grapefruit Posset

Raspberry and Mango Pavlova

Hot Rhubarb Soufflé

Gooseberry Custard Streusel Cake

Gooseberry and Elderflower Fool

Gluten-Free Churros with Chocolate Sauce

Buttermilk Panna Cotta

Bougatsa with Honey Poached Figs

Blueberry and Coconut Tarte

Whole Orange Polenta and Almond Cake

Lime and Coconut Drizzle Cake

Baked Peaches with Almonds with Marsala Cream

Peach Melba Upside Down Cake

Genoise Sponge with Raspberries and Lemon

Strawberry Polenta Cake

Mango Muffins

Chocolate Fudge Cake with Fudge Frosting

Oat and Sultana Cookies

Malted Milk Biscuits

Farmer Cheese and Sirniki Russian Cheese Pancakes

Eccles cakes

Bread and Baking

Pesto and Mozzarella Garlic Bread
Cheese and Spring Onion Scones
Chilli and Cheese Hot Cross Buns
Hot Cross Buns
Focaccia

Speciality Items
and Gift Ideas

Elderflower Cordial
See Pickled Cucumber